VOLUME 1

GRIFFON-POWERED

MUSTANGS

BY A. KEVIN GRANTHAM AND NICHOLAS A. VERONICO

specialtypress
PUBLISHERS AND WHOLESALERS

Published by
Specialty Press Publishers and Wholesalers
11605 Kost Dam Road
North Branch, MN 55056
United States of America
(651) 583-3239

Distributed in the UK and Europe by
Airlife Publishing Ltd.
101 Longden Road
Shrewsbury
SY3 9EB
England

ISBN 1-58007-034-5

Designed by Dennis R. Jenkins

Printed in the United States of America

Front Cover: *The Griffon was changed in August during the team's attempt to set the propeller-driven aircraft speed record, and when the racer arrived at Reno '79 the smart money was on the* Red Baron *and pilot Steve Hinton.* (Dave McCurry)

Back Cover (Left Top): *The finished product with Bill Rogers sitting in* Miss Ashley's *cockpit. B.F. Goodrich painted the aircraft with paint that was supplied by Courtaulds Aerospace.* (Rogers Collection, circa 1996)

Back Cover (Right Top): *Main-pressure oil feed to the crankshaft is directed through the inboard oil-gallery pipe that supplies main-pressure oil through the drilling and transfers ferrules in the reduction gear casing.* (Rolls-Royce)

Back Cover (Lower): *Running up the Griffon in* World Jet *at Phoenix '95. This view shows how far back the Griffon sits on the Mustang fuselage.* (Scott E. Germain)

TABLE OF CONTENTS

DEDICATION

This book is dedicated to the memory of Gary Levitz

PREFACE

AND ACKNOWLEDGMENTS

Unlimited class air racing is a sport with no equal. Some people believe Indy car racing is a close comparison, but Indy cars turn the track at only half the speed of an Unlimited Gold racer. Today, there is only one venue for air racing — the National Championship Air Races, held each September in Reno, Nevada. Attendance for the four-day event exceeds 150,000 spectators.

Over the years, spectators have seen the face of racing change from stock, ex-military aircraft to highly modified, purpose-built racers. Griffon-powered racers represent the ultimate in liquid-cooled racing technology. P-51 Mustang and purpose-built fuselages coupled with the Griffon exemplify the most horsepower and the smallest frontal area of any racer. This combination is reliable enough to defeat the horsepower monsters — clipped-wing Bearcats with R-3350s, as well as Corsairs and Sea Furys with 28-cylinder R-4360s.

In the 36 years of Reno racing to date, liquid-cooled Merlin- and Griffon-powered racers have taken the Championship, or Gold race, flag 19 times. Winners of the National Championship Air Races belong to an exclusive club — its roster currently has 17 names: Mira Slovak, Darryl Greenameyer, Clay Lacy, Gunther Balz, Ken Burnstine, Lyle Shelton, Lefty Gardner, Steve Hinton, John Crocker, Mac McClain, Skip Holm, Ron Helve, Neil Anderson, Rick Brickert, "Tiger" Destefani, John Penny, and Bruce Lockwood.

Everyone wonders who will be the next winner, and what new racers will show for the next season's events. This volume is an historical record of the Griffon-powered racers that have come before us, and will hopefully motivate others to build the ultimate racer.

Many in the racing community extended a warm reception and gave freely of their time to assist the authors with the preparation of this volume. We would like to recognize the kindness and generosity of Bill Rogers and the entire *Miss Ashley II* racing family including Dick and Mary Aley, John Brooks, Gordon Cole, Mike Gullikson, Greg and Sheryl Kerkof, Bob and Deanna Manelski, Jim Parks, Lance and Gayle Paxton, Hank Puckett, Bob Rogers, Dale Stolzer, and Brett and Mike Wilson for their support of this project. A special thank you is owed to Bill Rogers, Dick Aley, and Bob Manelski for their untiring technical assistance in helping us document *Miss Ashley II*'s racing history. A personal debt of gratitude is also owed to our very good friend John Brooks for everything that he did to make this book possible.

To the *Miss R.J.*, *Roto-Finish Special*, *Red Baron* family, many thanks to Chuck Hall, Gunther Balz, Randy Scoville, Pete Law, Darryl Greenameyer, and Steve Hinton.

We would also like to offer our thanks and appreciation to: Jackie Grantham, Holly Amundson, Betty Anderson, Richard Allnutt, Chuck Aro, Shawn Aro, Caroline and Ray Bingham, Darlene and Roger Cain, Ed Davies, John Davis, Jill Dunbar, Jim Dunn, Scott Germain, Wayne McPherson Gomes, Karen B. Haack, Todd Hackbarth, Ervan Hare, Earl Holmquist, Norm Jukes, John Kirk, Tillie and William T. Larkins, David McCurry, Thomas Wm. McGarry, Paul Neuman, Dan O'Hara, Dave Ostrowski, Dick Phillips, the staff of the Rolls-Royce Heritage Trust, Doug Scroggins, Kevin Smith, Becky and Ron Strong, Scott Thompson, Armand H. Veronico, Kathleen and Tony Veronico, Tim Weinschenker, Graham White, and Brett Wilson for their photographic and technical support. Thanks are also due to the Northern California Chapter — Library — American Aviation Historical Society, and the staff of Specialty Press.

We would like to offer our sincerest gratitude to the late Gary Levitz for giving us unlimited access to *Miss Ashley II*'s pit area and for three decades of great racing.

In addition, we shall be eternally grateful to Bill Stead for having the vision to revive the air races in 1964.

A. Kevin Grantham
Frederick, Maryland

Nicholas A. Veronico
San Carlos, California

THE HEART 1 OF A RACER

The engine is the heart of any air racer because power is speed and speed is the name of the game in racing. The contemporary aircraft that compete on the pylon course each year at the Reno National Championship Air Races are typically driven by engines that were developed during the first half of the twentieth century. These engines carry familiar names like Allison, Merlin, and Centaurus.

Air-cooled, radial power plants used for air racing come from one designer: Pratt & Whitney. Radial engines are generally referred to by the letter "R" which precedes a series of displacement figures such as R-2800, R-3350, and R-4360. However, there have been a few airplanes in racing history that have broken ranks with the aforementioned engine types and adopted the mighty, but extremely reliable, Rolls-Royce Griffon as their power plant of choice.

The genesis of the Griffon engine began shortly after Nazi Germany invaded Poland in 1939In response to German aggression, the British Fleet Air Arm sent a request to the famous engine manufacturer Rolls-Royce to develop a more powerful aircraft motor suitable for naval use. It was further specified that the dimensions and configuration of the new design should be compatible with existing military aircraft. That is, the design of Griffon should be such that it could be easily installed in airplanes that were presently using the Rolls-Royce Merlin engine. *Flight* magazine reported, "It would seem well-nigh impossible that with such similarity of overall dimensions in two engines of the same basic type, the swept volume of one should be 35.9 percent larger than that of the other. Such, however, is the case. Piston area of the Griffon is 23 percent greater than that of the Merlin, this having been achieved by increasing the cylinder bore to 6 inches, a figure which is just about verging on the optimum limit."*

Typical naval airplanes are built to withstand the riggers of an arrested landing on the moving surface of an aircraft carrier. The fighters and bombers that perform such duty take a beating each time they touch the deck of a ship and, as a result, these aircraft must be built with greater structural strength than that required of a normal airplane. Greater structural strength translates into a heavier airplane that will require more power to perform the same mission as an equivalent land-based aircraft.

Development work on the Griffon engine began in December 1939. Rolls-Royce reached back into histo-

---

*Reproduced with permission of the editor of *Flight Magazine*. Issue date May 7, 1954.

The Griffon design engineers copied many of the features that were used on the Rolls-Royce "R" engine that powered the Supermarine S-6 Schneider Trophy racer. (Rolls-Royce)

Griffon vs. Merlin
Specification Comparison of a Griffon Mk.69 vs a Merlin Mk.66

Specifications	Griffon Mk.69	Merlin Mk.66
Type	12 cylinder "V" 60 degree	12 cylinder "V" 60 degree
Construction	Two-piece aluminum alloy crankcase with two aluminum cylinder blocks (steel cylinder liners) and removable heads. Two inlet valves and two sodium-cooled exhaust valves per cylinder. Six throw one-piece counterbalanced crankshaft supported in seven plain bearings. Spur reduction gear, ratio 0.451:1.	Two-piece aluminum alloy crankcase with two aluminum cylinder blocks (steel cylinder liners) and removable heads. Two inlet valves and two sodium-cooled exhaust valves per cylinder. Six throw one-piece counterbalanced crankshaft supported in seven plain bearings. Spur reduction gear, ratio 0.477:1.
Supercharger	Gear-driven 2-stage 2-speed, ratios 5.84:1 and 7.58:1.	Gear-driven 2-stage 2-speed, ratios 5.79:1 and 7.06:1.
Carburetion	Roll-Royce Bendix/Stromberg 9T-40-1 three-barrel injection type updraft carburetor.	Roll-Royce Bendix/Stromberg 8D-44-1 two-barrel injection type updraft carburetor.

Dimensions		
Bore	6.00 in.	5.40 in.
Stroke	6.60 in.	6.00 in.
Displacement	2,240 cu. in.	1,649 cu. in.
Width	29.5 in.	29.8 in.
Height	46.0 in.	45.1 in.
Length	81.0 in.	78.0 in.
Frontal Area	7.9 sq. ft.	7.5 sq. ft.
Weight	2,075 lb.	1,650 lb.

Performance		
Take-off	1,900 hp, 2,750 rpm, 72.6 in. Hg.	1,320 hp, 3,000 rpm, 54.3 in. Hg.
Military Low	2,000 hp, 2,750 rpm, 6,750 ft.	1,705 hp, 3,000 rpm, 5,750 ft.
Military High	1,810 hp, 2,750 rpm, 21,000 ft.	1,580 hp, 3,000 rpm, 16,000 ft.
Normal Low	1,480 hp, 2,600 rpm, 13,500 ft.	1,400 hp, 2,850 rpm, 9,259 ft.
Normal High	1,350 hp, 2,600 rpm, 26,000 ft.	1,310 hp, 2,850 rpm, 19,000 ft.
Cruise Low	1,305 hp, 2,400 rpm, 12,250 ft.	1,305 hp, 2,400 rpm, 12,250 ft.
Cruise High	1,215 hp, 2,400 rpm, 25,000 ft.	1,040 hp, 2,650 rpm, 20,500 ft.

ry and resurrected the concept that was employed on the Schneider Trophy "R" engine. Namely, the same 60 degree V-12 configuration was used with 6.0-inch bores and 6.6 inch stroke with a total displacement of 2,240 cubic inches. In addition, Rolls-Royce came up with the idea of taking the camshaft and magneto drives off the front of the engine rather than from the rear as in previous designs. This innovation helped the engine builder keep the length of the power plant within the Fleet Air Arm's guidelines of being a direct replacement for the Merlin.

Driving the accessories off the front of the engine also reduced the torsional vibration in the camshaft drive. This was accomplished by using a "semi-floating coupling" to interface the camshaft drives to the crankshaft. The internal crank lubrication delivery system was another

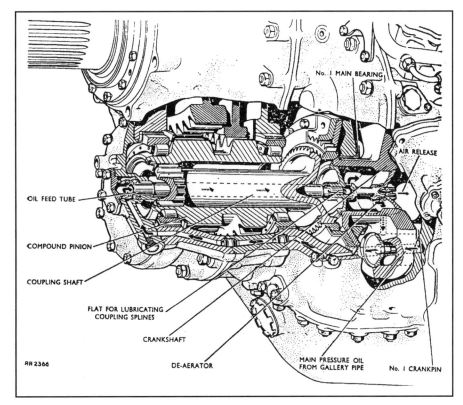

OIL FEED TUBE

COMPOUND PINION

COUPLING SHAFT

FLAT FOR LUBRICATING
COUPLING SPLINES

CRANKSHAFT

RR 2368

DE-AERATOR

No.1 MAIN BEARING

AIR RELEASE

MAIN PRESSURE OIL
FROM GALLERY PIPE

No. I CRANKPIN

The Griffon designers also exploited the two-stage blower section used on the Merlin. Both single-stage, two-speed and two-stage, two-speed superchargers were employed on the Griffon engine series. In the later types, a contra-rotating propeller setup was also developed to negate the effects from the engine/propeller torque.

The Rolls-Royce Griffon design had the longest military service life of any engine that emerged from the shadows of World War II. Its 50 year span, starting with the Fairey Firefly in 1941 and ending with the Royal Air Force's retirement of its Avro Shackleton maritime patrol bombers in 1991, empirically proved the power and reliability of Rolls-Royce's 1939 design.

Main-pressure oil feed to the crankshaft is directed through the inboard oil-gallery pipe that supplies main-pressure oil through the drilling and transfers ferrules in the reduction gear casing. The pressure oil in the crankshaft lubricates all main bearings through jets and radial drilling in the journals. (Rolls-Royce)

important design permutation of the Griffon. Rolls-Royce adopted an old idea of lubricating the main bearing by pumping oil through a hollow crankshaft. This approach not only reduced the number of external oil lines that were needed, but also

proved to be a better way of lubricating the overall crankshaft and associated components. In the end, the Griffon's internal oil delivery system was permanently adopted on all of Rolls-Royce's future piston engine designs.

The vigor and dependability of the Griffon engine is what first attracted the attention of the air racing crowd during the early 1970s. Merlin engine failures were commonplace in the early Reno days, so the opportunity to replace the Griffon's older brother with a longer lasting and more powerful substitute was an easy solution to the problem for three racing teams. The first Reno competitor to sport a Griffon was

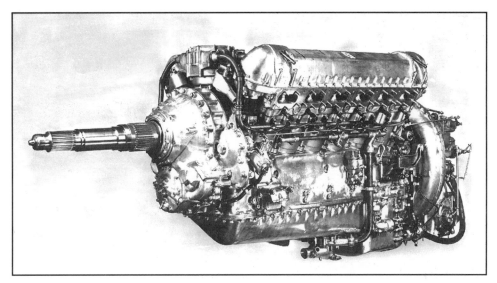

The Griffon 61 is similar to the Mk.74 series. Both engines were equipped with two-speed, two-stage superchargers. (Rolls-Royce)

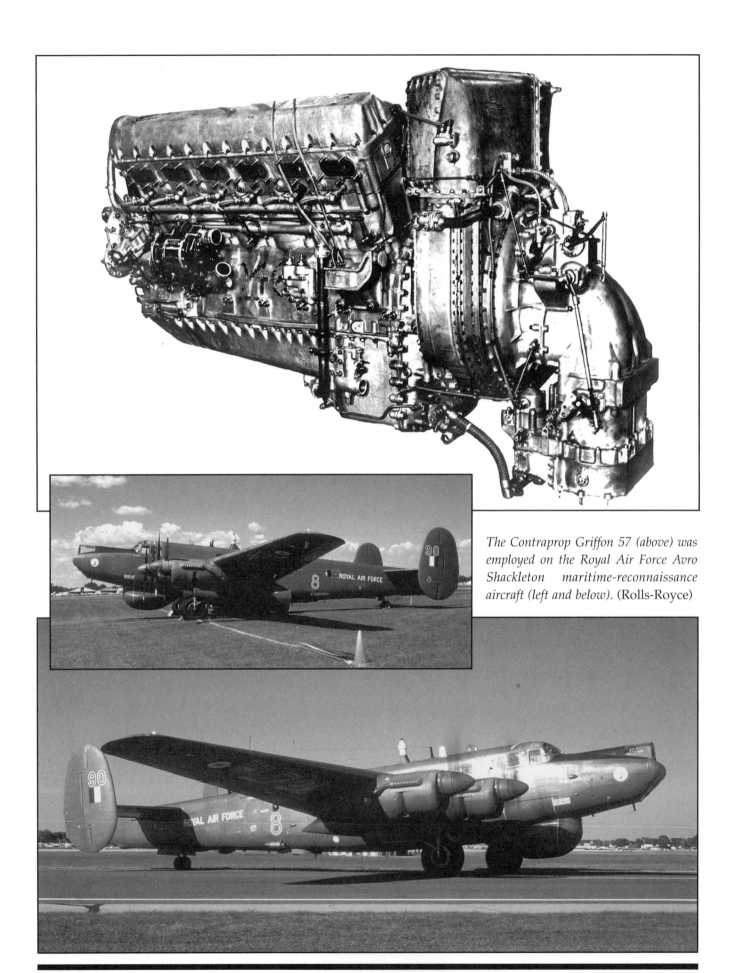

The Contraprop Griffon 57 (above) was employed on the Royal Air Force Avro Shackleton maritime-reconnaissance aircraft (left and below). (Rolls-Royce)

RACEPLANE**TECH**
S E R I E S

the RB-51 Mustang known as the *Red Baron*. This particular racing plane dominated the sport of air racing in 1977 and 1978, and set a world speed record of 499.018 mph in 1979. Ten years would pass before the next Griffon-Mustang variant made its racing debut. The Wittington brothers' *World Jet* competed in 1988 and in 1995. Then in 1997, the Levitz/Rogers' *Miss Ashley II* rounded out the trio of Griffon powered Mustangs to compete in the National Air Races.

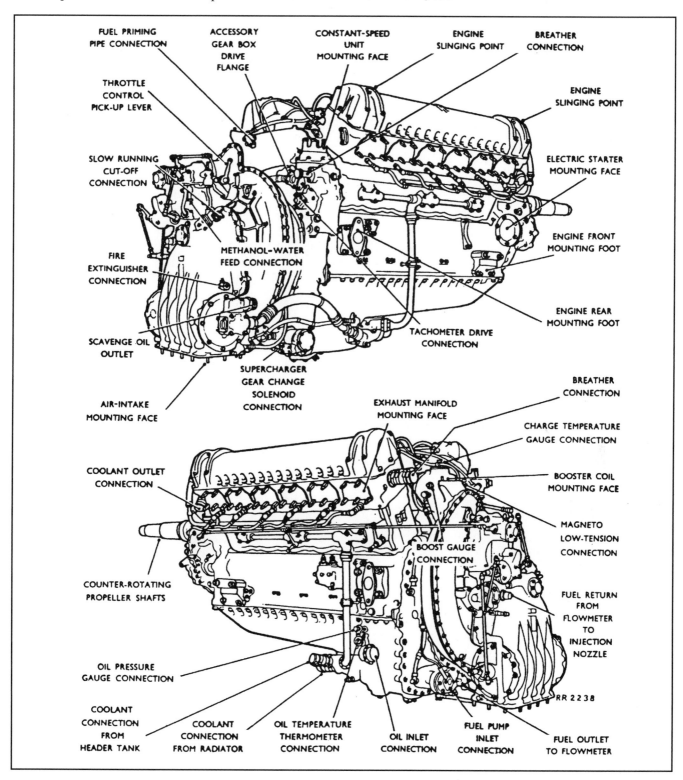

Connection points for the Griffon 57 - 59 series engine. (Rolls-Royce)

Early Griffons — the II, III, and IV — had two-speed, single-stage blowers, and gave a maximum power of 1,735 hp at 16,000 ft.(with high blower), and 1,495 hp at 14,500 ft. (with low blower). For take-off, 1,720 hp was available. These engines differed in reduction gear ratio, the II and III being geared 0.451:1, and the IV, 0.510:1. Until superseded by the Griffon XII, the series II engine was installed in the Firefly I and II; the Griffon III and IV were mounted in the clipped-wing Spitfire XII — specially developed to tackle the Fw-190 at low and medium levels. By increasing boost pressure to 15 lb./sq. in., the take-off power of the Griffon VI was raised to 1,815 hp — an increment of importance in that this engine powered the Seafire XV and XVII carrier-borne fighters. The Griffon XII resembled the VI except in supercharger and reduction gear ratios; it delivered 1,645 hp at 11,500 ft.

The system of designating the two-stage supercharged Merlins with series numbers beginning with "6" was also adopted for the Griffon range. For a weight increase of 290 pounds accounted for by the new blower system, the Griffon 61 delivered 2,035 hp at 7,000 ft., and 1,820 hp at 21,000 ft.; its most famous application was the Spitfire 21. Identical in all but reduction gear, the Griffon 65 powered the Spitfire XIV, and the Griffon 66 was again similar but had a cabin supercharger for photo reconnaissance work in the Spitfire XIX.

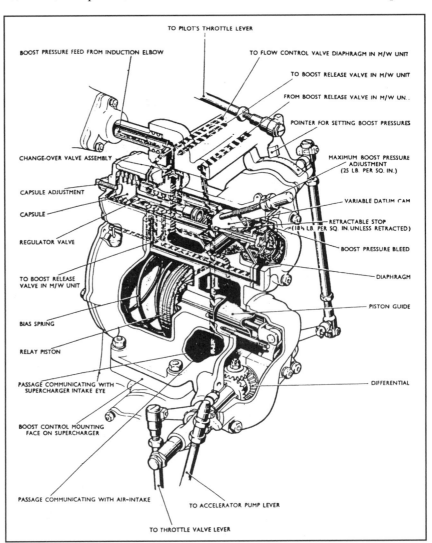

The automatic boost control is a mechanically-operated servo unit that operates the throttle valve in conjunction with the pilot's lever to control the boost pressure. It uses the pressure difference across the supercharger to limit the maximum boost pressure and to maintain the pilot's choice of boost pressure up to the capacity of the supercharger. (Rolls-Royce)

Griffons 64 and 67 were derived, respectively, from the 61 and 64, and gave no less than 2,375 hp at 1,250 ft. and 2,145 hp at 15,500 ft.; the 64 powered the Spitfire XXI and Seafire 46m, and the 67 appeared in the Spitfire XIV.

Though early examples of the Vickers-Supermarine Spitfire carried the Griffon 61, the production model had the Griffon 69 — the maximum power of each exceeded that of the earlier two-stage Griffons by some 300 hp,

with no increase in weight. This meant that each cylinder was developing something approaching 200 brake horsepower. Official maximum powers were 2,375 hp at 1,250 ft. in M.S. gear, and 2,130 hp at 15,500 ft. in F.S. gear.* Boost pressure was plus 25 lb./sq. in., made possible by 150 grade fuel.

Griffons 72 and 74 were further developments of the 65 for the Fleet Air Arm; they delivered 2,245 hp at 9,250 ft. The 74 was distinguished from the 72 in having a Rolls-Royce injection pump instead of the Rolls-Royce Bendix/Stromberg carburetor. These engines were, respectively, the power plants of the prototype Firefly IV and production Fireflies of the same mark.

An innovation of more than usual interest was a change made on the Griffon 85 involving contra-rotating airscrews; this engine appeared in the Spitfire XIV, XXI, and Seafire 45. The Griffon 87 was a further development, rated at 2,145 hp maximum at 15,500 ft., and the 88 differed only in having an injection pump. "Contraprop" Griffons, of the 85, 87, and 88 series, were mounted in the Spitfire XIV and XXI, and Seafire 45 and 47.

For the Barracuda V, Rolls-Royce developed the Griffon 37 with a modified two-speed, single-stage blower, maintaining 18 lb./sq. in. boost in either gear. Though the Barracuda was thus provided with no less than 2,055 hp at 2,250 feet, only Merlin-powered machines of this type went into squadron service.

---

*Rolls-Royce used the nomenclature of MS and FS to denote blower speed; i.e. MS is moderate speed and FS is fast speed. Same as low blower and high blower.

The Griffon Engine Fuel System Diagram. (Rolls-Royce)

Perhaps the most impressive of all Griffon developments was the three-stage supercharger incorporated in the 101 series, together with Rolls-Royce fuel injection. The new blower made possible an output of more than 2,000 hp up to 20,000 ft. — with no increase in dimensions. Weight rose by a mere 40 pounds.

Notable among postwar developments is the Griffon 57 for use in long-range patrol aircraft and having provision for contra-rotating airscrews. On this engine water-methanol injection is automatically brought into play when the boost pressure for the standard fuel approaches maximum value. The controlling unit works in conjunction with the boost control and progressively increases the flow of water-methanol with boost pressures from 18 to 25 lb./sq. in. Contraprop Griffons powered the Avro Shackleton maritime-reconnaissance aircraft. Other variants of the Griffon served in the numerous marks of Fairey Firefly.

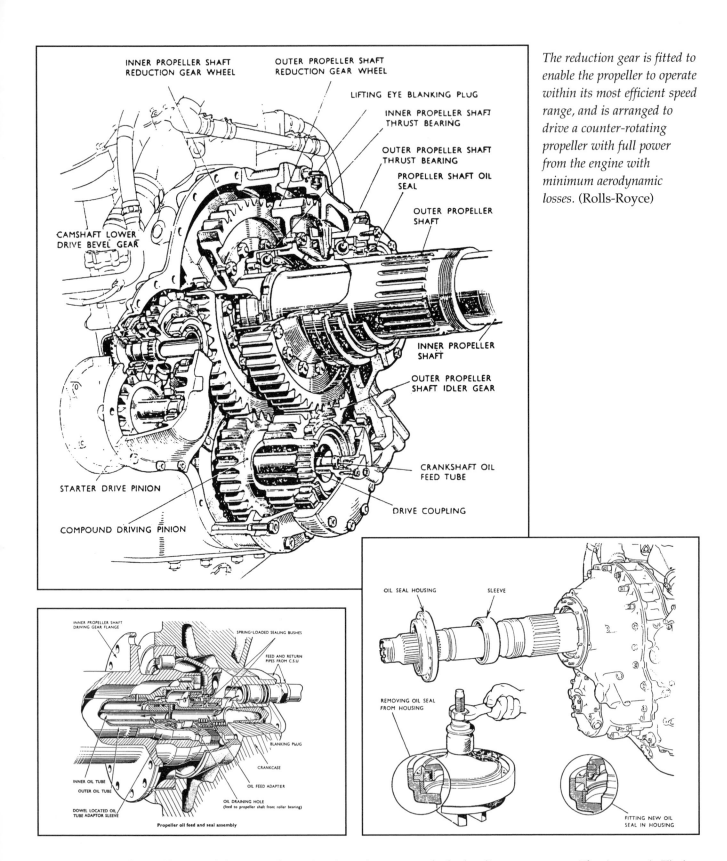

The reduction gear is fitted to enable the propeller to operate within its most efficient speed range, and is arranged to drive a counter-rotating propeller with full power from the engine with minimum aerodynamic losses. (Rolls-Royce)

INNER PROPELLER SHAFT REDUCTION GEAR WHEEL

OUTER PROPELLER SHAFT REDUCTION GEAR WHEEL

LIFTING EYE BLANKING PLUG

INNER PROPELLER SHAFT THRUST BEARING

OUTER PROPELLER SHAFT THRUST BEARING

PROPELLER SHAFT OIL SEAL

OUTER PROPELLER SHAFT

CAMSHAFT LOWER DRIVE BEVEL GEAR

INNER PROPELLER SHAFT

OUTER PROPELLER SHAFT IDLER GEAR

CRANKSHAFT OIL FEED TUBE

STARTER DRIVE PINION

DRIVE COUPLING

COMPOUND DRIVING PINION

INNER PROPELLER SHAFT DRIVING GEAR FLANGE

SPRING-LOADED SEALING BUSHES

FEED AND RETURN PIPES FROM C.S.U

BLANKING PLUG

INNER OIL TUBE

OUTER OIL TUBE

CRANKCASE

OIL FEED ADAPTER

DOWEL LOCATED OIL TUBE ADAPTOR SLEEVE

OIL DRAINING HOLE
(feed to propeller shaft front roller bearing)

Propeller oil feed and seal assembly

OIL SEAL HOUSING

SLEEVE

REMOVING OIL SEAL FROM HOUSING

FITTING NEW OIL SEAL IN HOUSING

Main pressure oil, in addition to lubricating the engine, is used to operate the hydraulic servo systems. The Automatic Timing Device uses main pressure oil, but the supercharger gear change servo and constant speed unit servo for the propeller operating mechanism use booster pumps to further increase the pressure. The oil seals prevent mixing of boosted pressure oil and main pressure oil, but slightly leaks oil past the outer seal. This oil then drains into the bore shaft and flows forward to lubricate the inner propeller front roller race. (Rolls-Royce)

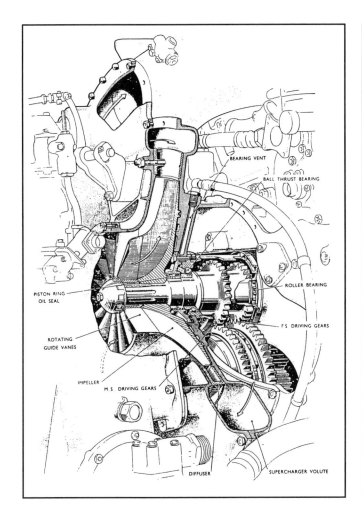

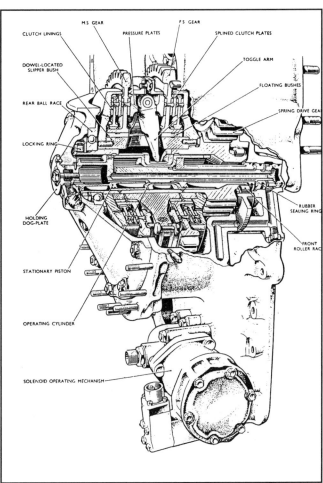

The super charger increases the power at altitude by compressing or boosting the charge before it enters the cylinders. (Rolls-Royce)

Supercharger Gear-Change Mechanism. (Rolls-Royce)

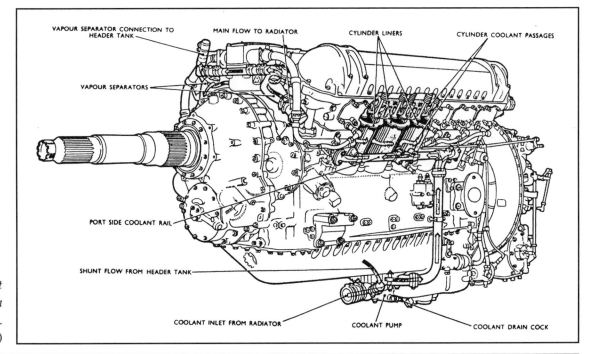

Engine Coolant System Diagram. (Rolls-Royce)

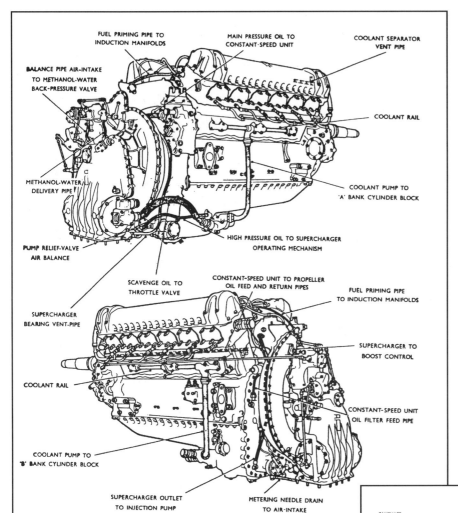

FUEL PRIMING PIPE TO
INDUCTION MANIFOLDS

MAIN PRESSURE OIL TO
CONSTANT-SPEED UNIT

COOLANT SEPARATOR
VENT PIPE

BALANCE PIPE AIR-INTAKE
TO METHANOL-WATER
BACK-PRESSURE VALVE

COOLANT RAIL

METHANOL-WATER
DELIVERY PIPE

COOLANT PUMP TO
'A' BANK CYLINDER BLOCK

PUMP RELIEF-VALVE
AIR BALANCE

HIGH PRESSURE OIL TO SUPERCHARGER
OPERATING MECHANISM

SCAVENGE OIL TO
THROTTLE VALVE

CONSTANT-SPEED UNIT TO PROPELLER
OIL FEED AND RETURN PIPES

FUEL PRIMING PIPE
TO INDUCTION MANIFOLDS

SUPERCHARGER
BEARING VENT-PIPE

SUPERCHARGER TO
BOOST CONTROL

COOLANT RAIL

CONSTANT-SPEED UNIT
OIL FILTER FEED PIPE

COOLANT PUMP TO
'B' BANK CYLINDER BLOCK

SUPERCHARGER OUTLET
TO INJECTION PUMP

METERING NEEDLE DRAIN
TO AIR-INTAKE

In addition to drilled passages in the engine casting, metal and flexible pipes are used to convey oil, coolant, and fuel. Standard nuts and nipples are used on all flexible pipes that are supported by clips to suitable points on the engine. (Rolls-Royce)

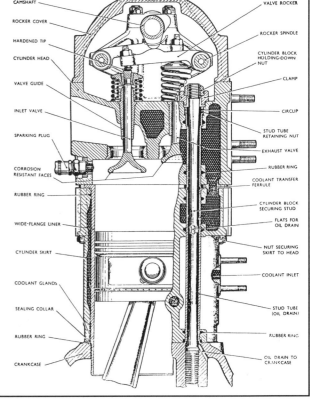

CAMSHAFT

VALVE ROCKER

ROCKER COVER

ROCKER SPINDLE

HARDENED TIP

CYLINDER BLOCK
HOLDING-DOWN
NUT

CYLINDER HEAD

CLAMP

VALVE GUIDE

CIRCLIP

INLET VALVE

STUD TUBE
RETAINING NUT

SPARKING PLUG

EXHAUST VALVE

RUBBER RING

CORROSION
RESISTANT FACES

COOLANT TRANSFER
FERRULE

RUBBER RING

CYLINDER BLOCK
SECURING STUD

WIDE-FLANGE LINER

FLATS FOR
OIL DRAIN

NUT SECURING
SKIRT TO HEAD

CYLINDER SKIRT

COOLANT INLET

COOLANT GLANDS

STUD TUBE
(OIL DRAIN)

SEALING COLLAR

RUBBER RING

RUBBER RING

OIL DRAIN TO
CRANKCASE

CRANKCASE

The cylinder blocks are among the most highly stressed parts of the engine. The wide-flange cylinder liners provide smooth bores that resist wear from the piston and rings. Four poppet valves, two inlet and two exhaust, in each cylinder head permit entry of fuel mixture and seals the combustion chamber during the compression and combustion strokes of the piston. The exhaust valves are hollow and are partially filled with sodium that helps cool the valve. (Rolls-Royce)

The first Griffon-powered aircraft to compete in an air race was a surplus Royal Canadian Air Force (RCAF) Supermarine Mk. XIV Spitfire (Serial Number TZ 138) in 1949. It was the first time since 1936 that the Cleveland, Ohio-based National Air Race Committee had allowed a foreign-built airplane to enter its pylon contests. This was also the first opportunity for most Americans to see an example of the famous British fighter, and speculation of how well it would do in the races ranged widely. The former military Spitfire was mostly untouched from its factory-delivered configuration, and the initial press releases claimed that the aircraft, with a top speed of 525 mph, was one of the fastest piston-powered aircraft in the world.

During the qualifying period, pilot James H.G. McArthur posted an average speed of 370.110 mph, which earned him $100 and the number six starting position for the Tinnerman Trophy Race. It also qualified the Spitfire as an alternate for the prestigious Thompson Trophy Race. Although 370-plus mph is a respectable speed, it fell far short of the 414 mph posted by top qualifier Dick Becker in his Goodyear F2G Corsair.

James H.G. McArthur was the first to race a Griffon-powered racer when he entered Supermarine Mk. XIV Spitfire TZ 138 in the 1949 Cleveland races. The ex-Royal Canadian Air Force Spitfire was essentially stock, and placed third in the 15-lap Tinnerman Trophy Race. (H.G. Martin photo from Robert J. Pickett Collection via Kansas Aviation Museum)

The competition that McArthur faced in the Tinnerman Trophy Race was formidable with three Lockheed P-38 Lightnings, two North American Mustangs (P-51A and P-51K), and a Goodyear F2G Corsair. The start of an air race, in the Cleveland days, was very exciting as all the participants lined abreast in a race horse type start for the 15-lap, 225 mile contest. When the starting flag was dropped, the pilots pushed the throttles to the stops and their racing planes reached for the scatter pylon. Howard Gidovlenko, piloting a modified P-38, was the first to pull out of the race in the third lap with engine problems. James Hannon's P-51A also left the course in the seventh. In the end, McArthur made a good showing by finishing third behind Ben McKillen's mighty R-4360 powered Corsair and Wilson Newhall's P-51K Mustang. The third place finish brought McArthur $1,050 in prize money. Not a bad weekend's earning for a gentleman pilot who was visiting Cleveland on a busman's holiday.

Rounding the pylons during qualifying, James H.G. McArthur flew the Mk. XIV to an average speed of 370.110 mph. Too slow for the Thompson Trophy Race, but an excellent competitor in the Tinnerman Trophy Race. (H.G. Martin photo from Robert J. Pickett Collection via Kansas Aviation Museum)

Red Baron Evolution

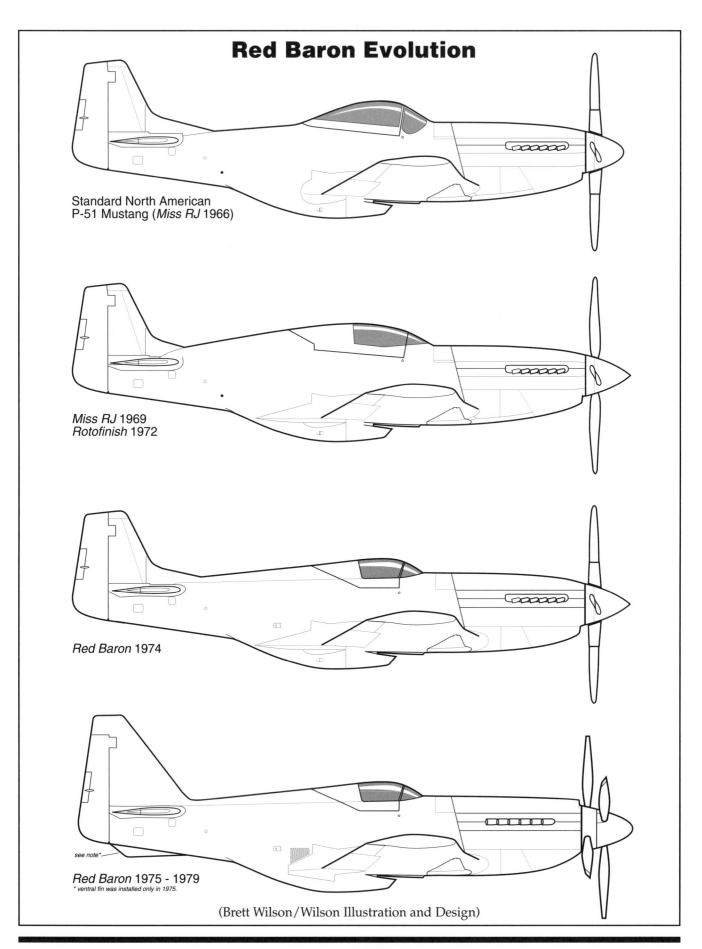

Standard North American
P-51 Mustang (*Miss RJ* 1966)

Miss RJ 1969
Rotofinish 1972

Red Baron 1974

Red Baron 1975 - 1979
see note
* ventral fin was installed only in 1975.

(Brett Wilson/Wilson Illustration and Design)

SETTING THE STANDARD FOR RADICAL RACING MUSTANGS

In the early 1960s, there was a national "need for speed." Drag racing and hot rodding had gripped the nation. Unlimited hydroplane racing was a huge sport drawing big-name sponsors and thousands of spectators to races at multiple venues. By 1964, young men who had grown up during the war years and had been captivated by the National Air Races — held each September in Cleveland, Ohio, from 1946 to 1949 — had matured into financially secure, adventurous businessmen. Many had chosen careers in military or commercial aviation, and for these pilots the ultimate adventure was flying surplus World War II fighters. They offered speed, aerobatics, and horsepower that could only be found in planes with names like Bearcat, Corsair, Sea Fury, and Mustang.

During the late 1950s, surplus military fighters could be purchased directly from the government or from aircraft brokers. At the time when a nice, three-bedroom, one-bath home sold for $14,000, a low-time, licensed, ready to fly P-51D was available for about $3,000. By 1964, the first year of air racing at Reno, Nevada, the price had doubled to more than $7,000.

Bill Stead, a Reno area rancher, entrepreneur, and 1958 and '59 National Hydroplane Champion, had been appointed to the Nevada Centennial Commission (1864-1964) — the perfect opportunity to find backing for his proposed National Championship Air Races. Stead was able to persuade the commission, the city of Reno, and the local chamber of commerce to back a nine-day

aviation event that would feature military displays with aerial demonstrations highlighted by the U.S. Air Force Thunderbirds, a transcontinental trophy dash, and pylon races in multiple classes including biplane, formula one, and a women's stock airplane race. A pylon racing class of surplus ex-military fighters, later to become known as the "Unlimiteds," would be the featured event. The first two years of the National Championship Air Races were held at the Sky Ranch, a small ex-military strip that bordered Bill Stead's ranch between Reno and Pyramid Lake.

In the summer of 1964, while preparations for the first National Air Races since the Cleveland days were getting under way, three friends — Frank Lynnott, Charles Willis, and

Miss R.J.'s first race outing was at Reno in 1966. Chuck Hall flew the stock Mustang to a sixth-place finish in the Consolation Race. (William T. Larkins)

Chuck Hall, bought P-51D N7715C from Capitol Airways of Nashville, Tennessee for $7,735. The aircraft was built at North American Aviation's assembly line at Dallas, Texas, and delivered to the Army Air Force as serial number 44-84961 on June 25, 1945. Built too late to see combat in World War II, the Mustang spent most of its military career with Air National Guard units in California, Wyoming, and Illinois. "I bought it to go have fun," said Chuck Hall. "In 1965, one of my partners was flying it and had an engine failure and bellied it in. I bought his interest out at that time."

After rebuilding the plane, Hall showed up at Reno 1966, the first year it was held at Stead Air Force Base — named for Bill's brother Croston, who perished while flying a Nevada Air National Guard P-51. Hall's stock P-51D, race number five, qualified at 283.77 mph, a conservative speed for the rookie racer. He finished sixth in the Unlimited Consolation race, but the racing bug had bitten him.* "I liked the excitement of racing — flying low, flying fast, and the competition among the other pilots," Hall said. "It was a very exciting, fast time."

During the off-season, Hall began an airframe clean-up and modification program. "We started doing extensive modifications to the engine and airframe. We modified the canopy, clipped the wings at the production break — taking about 3 feet off each wing. We then put Hoerner tips on it," Hall explained. An Aeroproducts propeller from a P-51H was also added, and the aircraft wore a new paint scheme consisting of an over-

all green with gold trim fuselage, rudder, and horizontal.

The 1967 Reno race eliminated heat racing. Once an aircraft had qualified, its speed determined whether it would compete in the consolation or championship race. Three F8F-2 Bearcats, one F4U-4, and six P-51Ds showed up to race. Hall qualified in fifth position at 373.47 mph — nearly 100 mph faster than the previous year. The championship race, held September 24, was 10 laps of an 8.04-mile course. During the first lap of the race, Chuck Lyford in the P-51D *Bardahl Special* dropped out with a broken piston. Darryl Greenameyer in the *Smirnoff* Bearcat crossed the finish line first at 392.62 mph, followed by E.D. Weiner in the P-51D *Hi Time II* at 373.71 mph. The

_____

* From its inception through 1979, the Unlimited Class Races were designated Consolation and Championship. In 1980, the now familiar Bronze, Silver, and Gold races were introduced.

By 1968, Hall had become a serious competitor. Crew chief Al Raines had fine-tuned the Merlin and a water-alcohol injection system had been added. The airframe also underwent an aerodynamic clean-up, and Hoerner wing tips were added. The aircraft has been repainted into an Eighth Air Force scheme. (William T. Larkins)

N7715C, Miss R.J., *was radically different when the racer returned to Reno in 1969. The military paint scheme had been replaced with an overall white and tangerine racing livery, a cut-down canopy, and extended spinner. During qualifying, the Merlin blew and Hall deadsticked the oil-soaked Mustang back to Stead Field. Hall replaced the modified Merlin with a stock engine and went on to finish second in the Unlimited Championship Race averaging 377.23 mph. (William T. Larkins)*

real race was for third and fourth position between Hall and United Airlines pilot Clay Lacy. Both P-51s were flying a close race, but Lacy edged Hall out of third with an average speed of 363.21 mph compared to Hall's 363.07 mph.

By Reno 1968, Hall's crew chief Al Raines had super-tuned the racing Merlin engine and a water-alcohol injection system had been added. Additional airframe clean-up had gone into making the racer as smooth as possible, and the plane wore the name *Miss R.J.* Qualifying for 1968 saw a new name in the pole position: Chuck Hall. He had flown the 8.5-mile course in 1 minute, 20.6 seconds for an average speed of 379.65 mph. Everything was going Hall's way. The field for the Unlimited Championship Race was two

F8F Bearcats flown by Darryl Greenameyer and Walt Ohlrich, and four P-51Ds raced by Hall, Weiner, Lacy, and Mike Loening.

As the race got under way Hall took the lead. Greenameyer had moved into second place, ahead of Loening. In the fifth lap, Loening's prop governor failed and his prop ran away. He was able to get the plane down safely, but as soon as he landed Weiner's engine quit having lost an 'O' ring in the induction system. Hall said, "I was leading right into the last lap, and in fact I was going down the home stretch, when a little 'O' ring in the prop governor failed and put the prop in high pitch leaving me with no control over the propeller." A 10 cent part cost Hall a first place finish. Greenameyer and Lacy passed Hall who crossed the

finish line third, ahead of Ohlrich. When the official results came in, Lacy was penalized for cutting number two pylon on the tenth lap, and Hall was moved into second place.

Having repaired the prop governor seal and returned home, Hall and his crew began a modification program. The stock windscreen and bubble canopy were replaced with a cut-down version; a lengthened, pointed spinner was added; and further modifications were made to the engine in the form of lighter, higher compression pistons. *Miss R.J.* now wore an overall-white with tangerine orange striped paint scheme.

During qualifying for 1969's Reno race, *Miss R.J.* blew the engine and Hall deadsticked (landed without power) the plane back at Stead

Field. Unable to change the engine and qualify in time, Hall was given time to install a stock Merlin and allowed to race from the 13th and final starting position. He would have to place third or better in the heat races to move up into the championship event — and that's exactly what Hall did. In Heat 2 on September 19, a five-lap race of the 8.5-mile course, Hall finished second at 358.65 mph, earning him a spot in the championship race field.

In the 1969 Championship Race, Hall would do battle with Darryl Greenameyer flying his Bearcat *Conquest I.* Greenameyer, who was at the top of his game, had qualified his Bearcat at 414.63 mph setting a new Reno qualifying speed, breaking his own record speed 409.97 mph that he had set in 1966. Rounding out the field were the Mustangs of Clay Lacy, Cliff Cummins in *Miss Candace*, and the Bearcats of Gunther Balz and Lyle Shelton. Hall and Lacy flew

another tight race, finishing second and third with average speeds of 377.23 and 371.70, respectively, but Greenameyer ran away from the pack. Greenameyer set a new Reno and National race record speed at 412.63 mph. Many in the racing community were wondering what it would take to beat the Bearcat.

The first year of the new decade saw Hall preparing the racer for the 1970 running of the National Championship Air Races. En route to the races, Hall was forced to land twice due to a rough running engine. During the qualifying runs at Reno, Hall blew another engine and was out of the races for the week.

Hall runs up the Merlin before qualifying at the California 1,000. Hall was one of the race's sponsors held at Mojave Airport, north of Los Angeles. The race involved 66 laps of a 15-mile course which was flown counter-clockwise. (William T. Larkins)

The beauty of the racer belies the violence of an engine failure. During the 20th lap, the Merlin broke its cam shaft forcing Hall out of the California 1,000 Race. (William T. Larkins)

Two months after Reno, on November 15, 1970, the California 1,000 Mile Air Race was staged at Mojave, California. The race was Greenameyer's brainchild and was also sponsored by Chuck Hall and Adam Robbins. Each lap was 15 miles long, turning around 10 pylons and would last for 66 laps. Unlike Reno, racers would fly the course in a clockwise manner — going fast, and turning *right*. Pit stops were allowed — actually encouraged — to provide action for the dozens of TV stations beaming coverage to the masses in nearby Los Angeles.

For this endurance race, Hall's crew removed the water-alcohol tank from behind the pilot's seat and installed a fuel tank to give the Mustang added range. *Miss R.J.* started the race in sixth place, but it just wasn't *Miss R.J.'s* year. In the 20th lap, the Merlin broke its camshaft forcing Hall to withdraw from the race. The aircraft sat at Mojave after the races had ended while a discouraged Hall gathered the money to replace, yet again, another expensive Merlin.

"I sold the airplane to Gunther Balz in 1971," Hall said. "I'd had about three engine failures, and it was getting very, very expensive. When the airplane was sitting out at Mojave it had some wind damage done to it, and I got a little discouraged and decided to sell it." Chuck Hall had been a tough competitor, but it was time to move on.

Gunther Balz: From Gentleman Racer To The Winner's Circle

Chuck Hall's loss of interest in N7715C, was Gunther Balz' gain. Balz ran Roto-Finish Company, a small, specialty industrial supplier of automation equipment for deburring machines in Kalamazoo, Michigan. "We used an airplane in our business to haul customers back and forth, and to visit their plants," Balz said. Roto-Finish had customers across the United States and licensees throughout the world.

"I was in the Navy for four years on a destroyer, and I didn't do any flying until I started as a civilian. I learned in a 65-horsepower Luscombe, and took to it. One thing lead to another and I bought an old, used T-6 and that was sort of interesting. Then the next thing you know, I had a Mustang. After I had a couple of Mustangs, I decided to try racing. I flew the early races with a Bearcat — as a gentleman racer. I thought that was kind of fun, and decided I would try and win it. So I went for a serious racer," Balz said. "The Bearcat is a much nicer airplane — more power, better handling. But for a serious racer, you really have to modify the Bearcat tremendously like *Rare Bear* or Greenameyer's airplane. There was a modified Mustang available and I decided to go that route." Balz acquired N7715C and painted the aircraft aluminum silver with black lettering, retained race number five, named it *Roto-Finish Special*, and began to improve on the modifications accomplished by Chuck Hall's crew.

"Hall had done some airframe mods and the engine had been tweaked a little bit, but we went a couple of more steps. In airframe clean-up you seal all the joints with putty, and put tape over all of the flap seals. Then the wing tips are cut off, the stabilizer tips are also cut off, and Hoerner tips are added to the wings. We extended the fairings on the trailing edge of the wing to the fuselage, installed a longer spinner, and cut the canopy way down, fairing it into the rudder — little things like that. Our team checked all of the systems, increased the engine power, and made it more reliable. The problem in racing is getting through a race and having it all hold together. It's a matter of attention to many, many details. And

Lyle Shelton's Able Cat *gave Chuck Hall some stiff competition during the heat races in 1969. In the Unlimited Championship, Hall finished nearly a minute ahead of and flew 40 mph faster than Shelton.* (Armand Veronico Collection)

Gunther Balz acquired N7715C from Chuck Hall in 1971. Balz gave the aircraft an aluminum-colored finish, and named it after his business — Roto-Finish Special. (William T. Larkins)

that's what we did. We got the details nailed down, and it held together through a race," Balz said.

Jack Hovey built the Merlin for the *Roto-Finish Special* using the banks and heads from the transport version of the Merlin, the 620, coupled with the V-1650-9 crankcase and supercharger. To keep the propeller tips from going supersonic at high RPMs, the reduction gear ratio was lowered. "What really counts is reliable horsepower," Balz said. But pushing an engine past its designed operating limits for 12 to 15 minutes is often an unanswerable prayer. Considering that stock military power in a P-51D is 3,000 rpm with manifold pressures at 61 in. hg. for takeoff and 67 in. hg. for war emergency power, Balz would be running 3,600 rpm and 120 to 130 in. hg. dur-

ing the Unlimited Championship Race. He had to push the Merlin to its extreme limits to catch the modified Bearcats rounding the pylons.

Balz brought the *Roto-Finish Special* to Reno 1971 ready to win. His team had put in a tremendous amount of effort and it showed during qualifying. This year was to be one of the fastest to date. For 1971, the course was extended from 8.5 miles to 9.8 miles and the championship race would last 10 laps. Balz qualified first at 419.50 mph and was followed by Lyle Shelton at 418.01 mph — both breaking Darryl Greenameyer's 1969 record-qualifying speed of 414.63 mph.

In the first heat race, Balz was facing the Mustangs of Howie Keefe (flying *Miss America*), Leroy Penhall, Roger

Wolfe, and Tom Summers, as well as the Sea Furys of Ormand Haydon-Baillie and Sherman Cooper. Balz was leading the race and near the end of the last lap when *Roto-Finish Special* lost its rudder trim tab. Balz pulled up and Keefe and Cooper passed beneath him to finish first and second. Meanwhile, Balz had his hands full. "The vibration was so tremendous, I thought I'd lost a prop blade," he said. "I was all set to bail out, but then it calmed down when I pulled the throttle back." Balz crossed the finish line at a high altitude, behind the grandstands in third position. He was credited with a third place finish by race officials, but no official time or speed was recorded. This caused great controversy at the time since Penhall would have been awarded a third place finish. While the race commit-

tee pondered its decision, Balz' crew replaced the trim tab in preparation for the championship race.

The field for the September 26 Championship Race saw four Mustangs, flown by Howie Keefe, Mike Loening, Leroy Penhall, and Gunther Balz, compete against the Bearcats of Greenameyer and Shelton, and the Sea Fury of Sherman Cooper. As the race got under way, Penhall cut pylon one on the second lap and that would cost him a time penalty. Seconds later Loening in P-51D *Miss Salmon River* blew its engine. He declared a Mayday, got the racer down safely, but had to ground loop the Mustang to get it stopped before he ran off the end of the runway. As the Mustang went around, the gear collapsed and the plane was badly damaged. Thankfully, Loening was unhurt. As the field began the last lap, Howie Keefe dropped out, also with a blown engine. He, too, declared a Mayday, landed safely, but was unable to stop in time and rolled out onto the runway overrun.

That left the Mustangs of Balz and Penhall slugging it out with the highly modified Sea Fury and Bearcats. Although he always flew a good race, Penhall was no competition. The race finished with Greenameyer in first, Shelton second, Cooper third, Balz fourth, followed by Penhall. The race was so close that only four-one-hundredths of a second separated the first and fourth place finishers. Greenameyer posted an average speed of 413.99 mph with Shelton turning in 413.07 mph — both Reno and National speed records. Cooper averaged 412.58 mph with Balz only a heartbeat behind at 412.10 mph. With his time penalty for cutting a pylon, Penhall's average time and speed was dropped to 15 minutes, 15.0 seconds at 385.57 mph.

Balz had pushed race number five as fast as it had ever gone, but still finished fourth. As Balz said, "What really counts is reliable horsepower." And in this race, each of the four finishers were developing nearly 3,000 horsepower. It was now a matter of reducing the *Roto-Finish Special's* aerodynamic drag, enabling it to go faster at the same horsepower.

Balz believed that was the key to beating the round-engined Sea Furys and Bearcats. During the off-season, Balz and his crew worked on further engine modifications and additional aerodynamic clean-up under the direction of Jim Larsen with Dwight Thorn as crew chief.

A Change in the Competition

NASA pilot Richard Laidley had gotten the nod to fly Darryl Greenameyer's Bearcat for Reno 1972 when Greenameyer had his license suspended by the FAA for violations while racing at Reno in 1971 — flying outside the race course, too near the pits and grandstand areas. Greenameyer had paid monetary fines to the race committee and retained his first place finish. His license was suspended after the race and he was banned from competing in 1972 by the Reno race committee. Laidley began practicing in July, and by race week was the odds-on favorite to win.

Laidley's stock as a race pilot went up even further when he qualified first at 411.19 mph. Flying his P-51D,

During a heat race at Reno '72, the Roto-Finish Special *lost a portion of the fiberglass on the right side of the fuselage.* (Karen B. Haack)

The fuselage, seen in the middle of the repair as the fiberglass sets, was quickly patched and Gunther Balz went on to win the 1972 Unlimited Championship Race. (Karen B. Haack)

Clay Lacy qualified second at 409.28 mph, followed by Lyle Shelton in his Bearcat at 402.74 mph. Gunther Balz posted the fourth fastest speed at 393.75 mph.

In the first heat race, Laidley dominated the field of two Mustangs, two Bearcats, a Sea Fury, and Bob Mitchem's modified FG-1D Corsair *Big Hummer*. In the second heat race, Balz and Lacy flew a tight race averaging 395.59 and 395.07 mph, respectively. During the race, a section of fiberglass on the right rear fuselage had peeled off, but Balz won the race and the fiberglass was quickly repaired and repainted in time for the championship race.

The seven plane race field for the 1972 Championship Race consisted of five aircraft that had demonstrat-ed the ability to be champions — the Bearcats flown by Laidley and Shelton, and the Mustangs piloted by Balz, Keefe, and Lacy. Rounding out the field were the aircraft of Mitchem, flying his FG-1D, and Ormand Haydon-Baillie, in his Sea Fury, that did not have the modifications needed to compete at speeds averaging 410 mph.

After the aircraft flew down the starting chute to begin the race, Laidley jumped out into the lead followed by Shelton, Balz, Keefe, Lacy, Mitchem, and Haydon-Baillie. Balz and Shelton were neck and neck, passing and repassing each other until the end of the third lap when the *Roto-Finish Special* blew past Shelton's Bearcat. "You've got to be willing to push the throttle awful far forward," Balz said. "I ran the RPM and manifold pressure up while running a lot of water-alcohol simultaneously with the doctored fuel — and just hoped it held together." Laidley was flying an extremely low race — to the point race officials and the FAA were worried he would catch a wing tip and cartwheel into the ground.

As the fifth lap began, the race had a new leader: Gunther Balz. He never looked back, and finished the race with a new Reno and National speed record of 416.16 mph. Laidley crossed the finish line second, but was disqualified for low flying. Shelton turned in an average speed of 404.70 mph, followed by Keefe at 398.53, Lacy at 380.89 mph, Mitchem at 341.99 mph, and Haydon-Baillie at 340.83 mph. "The biggest problem of the race was the parade lap in forma-

Jack Sliker taxies the Roto-Finish Special *out at Mojave in October 1973. Sliker placed fourth at an average speed of 348.483 mph. After the race, he sold the racer to Mac McClain's sponsor, Ed Browning.* (Veronico Collection)

tion with Bob Hoover. The problem is that you're burning up your fuel and water-alcohol supply and at race power you're running about 10 gallons a minute through the engine. So you hate to use it up sailing around the sky. After that race, I was down to fumes and had to land on the emergency runway," Balz said. "It's very hot in the cockpit. Racers cut the air supply down to reduce the drag – its extremely hot, and your adrenaline level is very high. You're suddenly very high, then afterwards you practically faint from fatigue." Having achieved his goal of winning the National Championship Air Races and doing it in the most highly modified Mustang of the time, and setting a speed record in the process, Gunther Balz retired from piloting unlimited racers. He would return to Reno in 1973 as team owner and continue to participate in the sport as a "gentleman racer."

For Reno 1973, John Wright was chosen to fly the *Roto-Finish Special*. He qualified fourth at 410.23 mph, placed fourth in the second heat race at 380.31 mph, and third in the championship race at 407.49 mph. Lyle Shelton won the race at an average speed of 428.16 mph — shattering Balz' record by more than 12 mph. Balz, who had enjoyed the spoils of victory, put the *Roto-Finish Special* up for sale. He said, "In 1973, we didn't have the same level of preparation, and I was glad to get

out of it without cracking up to tell you the truth." He returned to race at Mojave in 1973 in the Bearcat.

New Owners, New Team, New Spirit

Ownership of the *Roto-Finish Special* had passed to Jack Sliker, who brought the racer to Mojave for the 1973 races. At this point, Mojave had come to mirror the Reno races. Gone were the endurance races and the Unlimited Race was now ten laps of an 8.2-mile course. Lyle Shelton won the race in his Bearcat at an average speed of 381.482 mph. Sliker placed fourth at an average speed of 348.483 mph, nowhere near the airplane's potential. Sliker came to realize that the highly-modified Mustang was an extremely high maintenance airplane, and more than he wanted to deal with. Like Balz, Sliker enjoyed the flying qualities of the stock Bearcat. Sliker was a good friend of another racer named Roy "Mac" McClain who, with his sponsor Ed Browning, wanted to pursue a victory in the Unlimited Championship class. Sliker presented the *Roto-Finish Special* to McClain as the aircraft that could again win the race.

Taxing out at Mojave 1974, Mac McClain would earn the Red Baron's *first victory in a final-second dash past Lyle Shelton's Bearcat.* (Veronico Collection)

Ken Burnstine in Miss Suzi Q *taxies out at the October 1973 Mojave races. In 1975, Burnstine changed mounts to a new, highly-modified Mustang* Miss Foxy Lady. *Mac McClain in the Red Baron had to battle it out with Burnstine at Reno 1975.* (Armand Veronico Collection)

McClain was a Cessna Ag aircraft dealer and had been selling aircraft to Ed Browning who had a number of potato ranches up in Idaho. Browning knew that Mac had raced a T-6 and, ever the salesman, McClain talked Browning into sponsoring a race team and buying the *Roto-Finish Special* Mustang from Sliker. Browning and McClain acquired the aircraft in the middle of 1974, and it was flown to Eufaula, Alabama, McClain's home base. Here it was painted bright red and christened *Red Baron*, after Browning's Idaho Falls, Idaho, fixed-base operation Red Baron Flying Service. The Red Baron Racing Team would campaign the Mustang and an AT-6 as well.

It was quite a sight when the *Red Baron* showed up at Reno for the 1974 races. McClain and Browning had taken the "team" concept to a new level. The support trailer was painted to match the airplane and all of the team vehicles were lettered with the Red Baron Racing Team's name and logo. McClain qualified third at 417.33 mph, behind Shelton's new qualifying record speed of 432.25. In the first heat race, six laps of the 9.8-mile course, McClain flew the *Red Baron* around the pylons at an average speed of 400.37 mph — certainly competitive, but obviously saving the engine until the championship race.

The championship race field consisted of five Mustangs flown by John Wright, Korean War ace Bob Love in the *Oogahonk Special*, Ken Burnstine in *Miss Suzi Q*, "Lefty" Gardner in *Thunderbird*, and McClain in *Red Baron*. John Herlihy and Lyle Shelton flew the two Bearcats in the race. As Bob Hoover started the racers down the chute, Shelton, Love, and McClain were dueling it out — and it was going to get ugly. Before the end of the lap, McClain had declared a Mayday, pulled up off the course, and Love took his spot in second place. As McClain throttled back, his engine began to smooth out. He cancelled the emergency call and dropped back into the race, now at the back of the pack. He passed Herlihy and Wright, moving into fifth place.

As McClain was accelerating through the pack, the Merlin let go blowing the rods out the bottom of the engine and coating the windscreen in oil. McClain's flying skill brought the plane down safely, but it was a disappointing end to the *Red Baron's* first outing. While McClain was rolling out, the race continued above him. Shelton crossed the finish line first, and as second-place Bob Love was nearing the checkered flag, his engine went south and he started to pull up, declaring a Mayday. Next to cross the line was Burnstine in third place, followed by Gardner in fourth, with Herlihy and Wright closing out the race. And here's where it gets ugly: Shelton was penalized two laps for not pulling up to the required 300 feet during McClain's and Love's Maydays — thereby dropping him to fifth place (no time or speed was officially recorded); and the judges declared that Love was more than 500 feet above the course when he crossed the finish line — disallowing his second place finish, moving him to sixth place. Both Shelton and Love protested without success, and Ken Burnstine was declared the victor posting an average speed of 381.48 mph.

After the disappointing events of Reno, the Red Baron Racing Team headed for Mojave. McClain qualified third behind Shelton and Howie Keefe, and the championship race would be between this trio. When Hoover pulled up and the racers entered the course, Shelton and Keefe were leading McClain. The *Red Baron* quickly passed Keefe and

in a slow, deliberate manner, McClain closed the gap between himself and Shelton with each lap. As Shelton turned the last pylon and headed for the checkered flag, McClain poured it on. The *Red Baron* edged past Shelton, crossing the finish line a half second ahead of the Bearcat. The race was so close, Shelton had thought he'd won the race, but it was not so. The *Red Baron* had achieved its first victory.

Taking The Next Step: Red Baron and The Griffon Engine

While the Red Baron Racing Team was competing at Reno 1974, there was a meeting between Mac McClain, sponsor Ed Browning, engine builder Dave Zueschel, and Lockheed aerodynamicists Bruce Boland and Pete Law, to discuss what could be done to make the *Red Baron* a faster airplane. "Everybody there knew we would be talking about the installation of a Griffon

engine in a P-51. Chuck Lyford had talked about doing it for years," Pete Law said in an interview with air racing historian Tim Weinschenker. Boland was tasked with completing all of the aerodynamics — structures design and load calculations, as well as designing the engine mount. Dave Zueschel had Randy Scoville working for him and Mike Nixon as well. The three were tasked with the engine work.

By the mid-1960s Dave Zueschel had become legendary as a racing-engine

builder, building dragster engines as well as Merlins and Griffons for drag boats and unlimited hydroplanes. "I worked for Dave Zueschel for 10 or 12 years and during the last few years of working there we wound up with the *Red Baron* project," said Randy Scoville. "I was the lead engine builder in the shop and when Browning decided to put this thing in the airplane and do this project, he asked me if I wanted to be the crew chief also. I said, 'Yeah!' By osmosis I wound up becoming the crew chief and engine builder.

Tail view of the newly modified Red Baron at Aerosport. Note the amount of work done to the wings -- the tips have been clipped, ailerons shortened, and the gun bay area has been coated with bondo to improve the aerodynamic cleanliness of the wing surfaces. (Veronico Collection)

"I worked a long time with Dave Zueschel. We started out drag racing together — then I went to work for him. We drag boat raced and unlimited hydroplane raced, and unlimited airplane raced. We got into the airplanes in 1966 when I first hooked up with Dave." Zueschel was building dragster engines for Greenameyer, and hired Scoville to maintain the car. When they were at the track, Scoville worked for Greenameyer, and when the races were over he worked in the shop for Zueschel. At this point in time, Greenameyer also owned a Bearcat and a P-38. "We had a business where we built a lot of engines for top fuel dragsters and fuel drag boats. It started to wane as Dave's interest grew more and more toward airplanes," Scoville said.

During the 1974 races at Reno and Mojave, McClain came to the conclusion that he was having to run the *Red Baron's* engine way too hard chasing down the radial engine

Bearcats and some of the better performing Mustangs. "Historically the Mustangs have been at a disadvantage. When they hang together they win. When they don't, they're pretty spectacular blowing up," Scoville said. "What we needed was something bigger to give us more consistency so we didn't have to extract so much power from such a small powerplant. We knew of the Griffons having descended from the Rolls-Royce 'R' project (the Supermarine Schneider Cup Racers) and knew they were just starting to become available from surplus Shackletons. The English were phasing the Shackletons out at that time — the end of 1974 and the first months of 1975. We had dealt with a scrap dealer over in England buying Merlins. We contacted him about finding some Griffon stuff, and he called us back about two days later and asked how many we wanted. He said he could get us more Griffons in better condition than any Merlin he could ever find. We

wound up buying three Shackleton QECs — motor mount, propeller, spinner, everything.

"We decided that if we were going to absorb the Griffon's power, we should stick with the counter-rotating propeller but modified by cutting the diameter down. The contra-rotating propellers eliminated the engine's torque. The front end of the engine was real nice. Mk 58 Griffons were postwar engines so they had some very nice modifications when compared to a Merlin or even an earlier Griffon. The one thing they lacked was a two-stage supercharger. They only had a single-stage supercharger because they were in a patrol aircraft not a fighter.

"We looked at grafting the two — we had taken some single-stage Merlins and put later, two-stage blowers on them. With the Griffons it was the exact opposite as the earlier engines were two-stage – the MK 65, 66, and 74s from Fireflys and

Spitfires, so we wound up getting some –74 engines which were out of a Firefly. We took -74 backends — the wheel case, supercharger, and after cooler, and we grafted that to a –58 front end. The only change required was replacing the crankshaft adapter for the quill that drove the wheel case, supercharger, and after cooler. We had what we considered the best of both worlds — we had the bulletproof power section; late-model, late-engineered power section; counter-rotating nose case; and the back end with the two-stage after-cooled supercharger where it would pull boost at altitude."

The Griffon did not have a carburetor as it was equipped with a Hobson fuel injector (drum valve with an engine-driven pressure pump with a central spray nozzle in the back of the supercharger). The Hobson unit does not have any mass airflow correction and it senses mani-fold pressure through the throttle's position and then compensates for boost. A nice idea for a patrol bomber, but it would not work in a racer. In addition, there were no FAA approved shops maintaining the Hobson fuel injector at the time.

Pete Law, who did all of the fuel flow and thermodynamics calculations recommended using the PR58 carburetor. He said, "The Griffon engine is 2,239 cubic inches and an R-2800 is 2,800 cubic inches. We were going to be taking more air into the Griffon engine than was going through an R-2800 engine by quite a bit. We were intending to get 3,200 to 3,300 horsepower out of the Griffon and you have to take so many pounds per hour of air into an engine to get the horsepower — 7.3 pounds per hour of air per horsepower. If you want to make 3,300 horsepower you've got to be able to take 24,000 pounds per hour of air-flow through an engine. You can easily do that with a PR58 which is used on both the R-2800 and the R-3350.

"Knowing the fuel flow versus air flow relationship for the carburetor of the Griffon, I was able to convert the R-2800 carburetor's fuel flow. The PR58 took the airflow through it, metered it, put the right amount of fuel into the engine and it worked very well," Law said. He also adapted the R-2800's CB-17 water injection unit to the Griffon engine. The PR58 carburetor and CB-17 water-injection units were an excellent choice — the *Red Baron* never had carburetion problems.

To mock up the engine installation, Zueschel's team borrowed a bare Mustang fuselage from Aerosport. After leveling it, they used the fuselage as a fixture to build the motor mount. Zueschel's team put a Griffon engine on a set of jack screws,

The tail modifications are evident in this view. The tail's chord was increased and the offset removed. In later modifications the tail's height would be increased. (Veronico Collection)

The Red Baron's newly installed Griffon gleams while awaiting its time to turn over. To install the Griffon engine, the firewall had to be cut, the rudder pedals moved back one foot, and a down draft carburetor had to be fitted, forcing the supercharger case to be mounted against the lower firewall. (Veronico Collection)

rolled it up against the Mustang's firewall and then jacked it up to set the engine thrust line. Then they began designing and building the motor mount and cowling. It was a six-month project that had three to four people working on it. The go-ahead to build the airplane was given in January and it was flying at Mojave in June. "We wound up cutting the firewall out and moving the pedals back about a foot. One of the reasons for turning the rear of the supercharger over to make it a downdraft rather than an updraft carburetor is so we could get the back of the supercharger case right up against the lower edge of the firewall," Scoville said. This altered the *Red Baron's* appearance — the air intake was moved from below the nose case as seen on all Merlin-powered Mustangs to above the engine,

similar to the Allison-equipped P-51A. "That let the whole carburetor and the inlet elbow that's cast into the rear cover of the supercharger sit in the compartment where the electronic relays and the hydraulic reservoir were on a stock Mustang. When you took the panel off behind the firewall in the *Red Baron* you looked right down at the carburetor and the duct came in through there," Scoville explained.

The vertical thrust plane* of a stock Mustang was right between the *Red Baron's* two counter-rotating propellers. The rear propeller was aft and the front propeller forward of the stock Mustang's vertical thrust line — so it was right at the split line

of the contra prop. The horizontal thrust line was two inches lower than in a stock Merlin. "One of the reasons we moved the thrust line down was to accommodate a top inlet duct. We fudged that so we could run the duct over the top of the after cooler and over the top of the inlet trunk. It came up over the top of the spinner like an A-model Mustang," Scoville said. "That was all part of the scenario of having the fuselage and the motor on a trolley with jack screws to where we could jack either one up or down and mock-up the assemblies."

During the *Red Baron* project, Scoville and Law were also working on the Griffon installation in Bernie

* Vertical thrust plane is the plane of the engine's propeller where forward thrust is developed.

Little's Budweiser unlimited hydroplane. While the engine and fuselage were going up and down on the jack screws in an effort to mate the two, the *Red Baron* was flown to Dick Hairston's Aerosport at Chino, California, for the airframe modification. A number of people were involved in the work and they included: Roy Steen who did the machining of numerous parts and the engine mount; Doug Kruse who did the metal work on the nacelle; and Ray Poe who also worked on the engine mount. Dick Hairston was in charge of getting the airframe ready. He was assisted by Bob Carr, Jerry Morrison, and "Soup" Hoisington. Keith Bailey from West Coast Propeller worked to get the counter-rotating system working as well as trimming and balancing the propellers. Dick Evans of Evans Plastic built the canopy. Robbie Patterson, and Bill and John Muzala were mechanics on the airplane. John Muzala also flew the airplane — one

of only four pilots to fly it. Additionally, Al Dimauro, owner of the Aircraft Carburetor Company in Burbank, worked closely with Pete Law to complete the carburetor and water-injection systems.

Red Baron crew chief and engine builder Randy Scoville described the teamwork that went into the aircraft's conversion. "This project wasn't any one person — except for Ed Browning's pocket book. Bruce Boland and Pete Law worked in Burbank, and we were in Sun Valley, only five minutes away. They used to come by on the way home every night. We had this unlimited engineering group so to speak. When we had a problem, I can remember calling Pete and Bruce during the middle of the day a number of times, and they'd either give you the answer then, or they'd have the answer that evening on the way home — charts, graphs, instructions on how to do this or that. Then here

were a lot of things they were stuck on and we were able to help them — because we didn't know you couldn't do certain things. We just did it."

Having had such extensive modifications, the *Red Baron* was given a new type designation — the one and only RB-51.

1975 to 1979: Years of Domination

When the racers and spectators arrived for the first race of 1975, at Mojave, everyone was in awe of the *Red Baron*. What other teams had dreamed of, the *Red Baron* team accomplished — the installation of a Griffon in a Mustang fuselage. Many thought it would be unbeatable.

During the plane's modification, the tail was kept at the stock height and its one and one-half degree offset was removed because the counter-rotating propellers eliminated the torque, and the tail's

The Griffon roars to life. At this point, the crew could only dream of the success the racer would have at the hands of pilots Darryl Greenameyer and Steve Hinton. (Veronico Collection)

chord was increased. At Mojave, for the first time, *Red Baron* was wearing a ventral fin to increase longitudinal stability.

Mac McClain took the newly-modified racer out around the Mojave course and qualified at 401.52 mph. Not bad for the racer's first show-

ing. In the championship race on June 22, 1975, McClain flew down the slot behind the field and completed the first lap at 292.91 mph. He then pulled out of the race unable to keep the canopy latched. The entire team and many fans were disappointed.

After the race, "Mac said the plane had some adverse yaw characteristics so we added a ventral fin and increased the height of the vertical

Outside the Aerosport hangar at Chino Airport, the newly-installed Griffon engine and counter-rotating propellers come to life. (Dustin W. Carter Aeronautical Collection)

After the 1974 Reno races, the Red Baron *team began a radical modification program with the installation of a hybrid Griffon engine and counter-rotating propellers. The light areas of the fuselage show areas of new airframe modifications. (Dustin W. Carter Aeronautical Collection)*

Lyle Shelton's Rare Bear *not only holds the world piston engine speed record but is also, when it is running right, the plane to beat at Reno. This highly-modified Grumman F8F Bearcat is powered by a specially-built Wright R-3350 engine. (A. Kevin Grantham)*

by putting an 18-inch cap on the top of it," said crew chief Scoville. "It was taller than a P-51H model."

The racing circuit moved on to Reno in September, and McClain qualified in sixth position at 407.39 mph, 28 mph slower than pole sitter Darryl Greenameyer who turned the pylons at 435.56 mph.

In the championship race, McClain poured on the power as the racers went down the chute and, as he turned on the spray bar to cool the engine, the windscreen fogged up. McClain had no forward visibility and his spray bars were full on. This quickly depleted his supply of spray bar water and every second he came closer to overheating the engine. Although faced with the possibility of blowing a $40,000 Griffon, he made his way through the field and nearly caught front-runner Lyle Shelton. Unfortunately for McClain, the race ended too soon and he placed second at 427.313 mph, four seconds behind Shelton. Under the circumstances, the second place finish proved to many that the Mustang/Griffon match-up would be a winning combination.

McClain and the team were looking to avenge their 1975 Reno loss to Shelton at Mojave in 1976. Unfortunately, Shelton's Bearcat blew an oil line both times he attempted to qualify — the second attempt resulting in a belly landing that badly damaged the airplane. Shelton was out, the best competition for the *Red Baron* was grounded, and the team would have to wait for another race to defeat the Bearcat. McClain looked sharp as he qualified at 416.27 mph. Cliff Cummins and his modified P-51 *Miss Candace* were now the *Red Baron's* biggest worry.

The Unlimited Race started with Charlie Beck in P-51D *Candyman* jumping into the lead. That didn't last long as the *Red Baron* blew Beck back into the pack. Cummins who started the race in fourth position had moved into second and was putting the heat on McClain who had throttled back. Just as Cummins was attempting to pass, *Miss Candace's* Merlin let go. After an excited Mayday call, Cummins got the racer on the ground safely. *Red Baron* was so far ahead, the racer was behind it for second place. When the checkered flag dropped, McClain had

won the first race in a Mustang powered by a Griffon engine at a comfortable 406.718 mph. Gary Levitz took second place at 376.349 mph.

There was a charge in the air at Reno in September 1976. Everyone was expecting something big. During qualifying, the top three aircraft broke the Reno and National speed records — Don Whittington in P-51D *Precious Metal* flew the course at 438.81 mph; John Crocker in *Sumthin' Else* at 436.63 mph; and McClain in *Red Baron* at 436.09 mph.

Unfortunately, not everything turns out the way it's supposed to. The championship race was an all-Mustang affair. The racers included Whittington, Crocker, McClain, and Howie Keefe in *Miss America*, Darryl Greenameyer in *Flying Undertaker*, Jimmy Leeward in *Miss Florida*, and Clay Klabo in *Iron Mistress*. When things can't get worse, they sometimes do. John Crocker led the race from entry on the course to the checkered flag. He averaged 427 mph. Around the end of the first lap, his prop seal started to leak and covered his windscreen with a thin film of oil. For safety considerations,

Crocker flew the course high and wide, and crossed the finish line first. Air race officials believed he violated the race deadline on all eight laps by flying high and wide and disqualified him. In the third lap, about to pass McClain, Whittington's Merlin threw a rod and burned a couple of pistons. On the fourth lap, McClain's blower gears quit while chasing Crocker. In the sixth lap, Klabo's engine sprang a leak, and he, too, was out of the race. Howie Keefe lost an exhaust stack but was able to keep his engine together long enough to finish the race. Thus Gardner won at an average speed of 379.61, followed by Greenameyer, Keefe, and Leeward.

"McClain was a really good stick and rudder guy, but he wasn't much of an engineer," said Scoville. Until this time, McClain was the only pilot to have flown the *Red Baron*. The Monday after the 1976 Reno races ended, sponsor Ed Browning had had enough. Everyone on the team was putting in tremendous effort, yet they were not winning races. To

Browning it seemed the weak link was McClain. He asked Darryl Greenameyer to fly the airplane and tell the team what was wrong with it. "Darryl loved flying three-point takeoffs and landings — that way he kept his Bearcat's Skyraider blades from hitting the ground. They were too big and he *had* to make a three point takeoff and landing," Pete Law related. "On Monday, Darryl went roaring down the runway from left to right at Reno — from west to east, three point, lifts off, and he can't climb because he's at too high an angle of attack. The drag is too high. He's at full throttle as hard as he can push it, and it will only do so much. Off the end of the runway is Lemon Valley, and Darryl pushed the airplane over, diving into Lemon Valley to get enough airspeed so he could accelerate and climb. If that end of the runway had not gone off 200 or 300 feet, he would have had to put the airplane down in a field.

"Darryl takes off, flies it around and immediately lands. He said the *Red Baron* was the worst airplane for aft

CG (center of gravity) he'd ever flown. Everybody looked at each other in disbelief," Law said. Crew chief Scoville said of the flight's aftermath: "When Darryl told us that, I said, 'no, wait a minute,' and I drug out all the paper work and put the airplane on the scale. Darryl said, 'I don't care what it says, I'm telling you how it flies.' All of the sudden a big light bulb came on and everyone realized that we had lowered the thrust line, so the thrust cone was impinging the tail plane at a different attitude and it wasn't carrying the tail as much. We took the ventral off, removed a lot of now unnecessary weight, and the airplane just kept getting better and better."

After Greenameyer flew the airplane and McClain found out about it, he and Browning had a blow-out — and Mac quit the team. Steve Hinton, who would later fly the *Red Baron* to numerous victories said, "The funny thing was, it's like a lot of the hybrid airplanes — it wasn't tail heavy on paper but aerodynamically it was. It was designed as a modification to a Mustang, so it wasn't out of line that way. The problem lies in the fact that the thrust line of the engine was different and the wings were shorter. These are things we learned about as we did them. Everybody knows now because of airplanes like the *Red Baron* that went through that development."

Greenameyer Brings a Winning Tradition to the Team

Greenameyer was involved in building an F-104 to capture the low altitude speed record, but he signed on to fly the *Red Baron* for the 1977 season. This was a beneficial move as Browning decided to sponsor Greenameyer's F-104 efforts too.

After the successful run-up, the cowling is buttoned down in preparation for the aircraft first post-modification test flight at Chino Airport. (Veronico Collection)

The promoters of Mojave took 1977 off to regroup, making Reno the only unlimited event of the year. When the aircraft arrived on the Reno ramp, the wings were white with *Red Baron* in a Gothic script. Greenameyer qualified third at 385.15 mph, 6 mph faster than McClain who was now piloting P-51D *Escape One*. For the Unlimited Championship Race, Greenameyer's competition would be Whittington and Cummins, but he made short work of everyone in the race by turning an average speed of 430.703 mph. Whittington was close behind at 425.701 with Cummins at 424.357. Greenameyer had now won his seventh Unlimited Championship Race.

After basking in the victory, Greenameyer's contract to fly the plane was up, and it was time to look for a new driver. "Steve Hinton had been on the team as a mechanic, and I had gotten to know him pretty well after four or five years," Scoville said. "Before the *Red Baron*, he was out at Aerosport, he worked for Leroy Penhall, and Penhall was one of our customers at Zueschel's shop. Hinton was like we were with cars — except he was that way with airplanes. He and Jim Maloney grew up around airplanes. By the time Hinton had flown the *Red Baron*, he was more qualified than most race pilots. With his mannerism and 'no big ego,' you just didn't know it. Everyone thought he was another greasy kid working on the airplane.

"Darryl agreed to fly the plane in 1977, but he wanted to work on his F-104 project. Ed asked me, 'Who we gonna get to fly this?' I told him he was already working on the team — Steve. Ed was amazed. I told Ed that Hinton doesn't run his mouth about it, but I guaranteed this would be a piece of cake for him. And it was.

Red Baron Clipped Wing Design

Standard North American
P-51 Mustang Wing Design

Red Baron
Clipped Wing Design

Wings were clipped to the
next inboard structural rib.

(Brett Wilson/Wilson Illustration and Design)

Red Baron *on the ground at Reno '76. Note the ventral fin and increased height of the tail.* (Grantham Collection)

Bob Hoover flew as safety pilot in his bright yellow P-51D from the early days of Reno until the mid-1990s when the job was handed to Steve Hinton. Hoover coined the phrase, "Gentlemen, you have a race," as he released the field onto the course. (Nicholas A. Veronico)

Darryl gave him a little check-out in the airplane, he jumped in, and won the first time he ran it. He walked away from everybody."

To describe Steve Hinton's first season with one word, "alone" is it — alone at the top! The 24-year-old pilot arrived at Reno in 1978 with some big shoes to fill, those of Darryl Greenameyer. To prove he was the right man for the job, Hinton qualified at 427.15 mph — not a record, but more than 27 mph faster than his closest competitor Cliff Cummins in P-51 *Miss Candace*. The Unlimited Championship Race saw Lloyd Hamilton's Sea Fury *Baby Gorilla* battle it out with six other Mustangs. Weather-wise, race day was brutal. The wind was howling and snow was falling sporadically. Cummins was out of the race with a sick engine and Don Whittington in *Precious Metal* was to be Hinton's nearest rival. The two battled it out, trading first and second place repeatedly, but when it counted, Hinton was in the lead turning in a speed of 415.457 to Whittington's 414.766. Hinton had won his first race, and all thoughts of the *Red Baron's* previous pilot's winning ways were erased. A new championship dynasty was born.

A little more than one month later, the *Red Baron* team was in the high desert at Mojave and, for the second time that season, battling the elements — the wind. Early in the race week, the weather was fantastic. Hinton qualified at 408 mph and won the race at 371.28 mph. The season was over, the *Red Baron* and Hinton were two for two.

Don Whittington sponsored the first race of the 1979 season, and the venue was Homestead, Florida — south of Miami, held the first week-

end of March. Whittington in *Precious Metal* qualified second at 380 mph behind Hinton at 395. John Crocker in *Sumthin' Else* posted the third highest qualifying speed at 368 mph. Hinton easily won the race at an average speed of 384.791 mph.

With his third Unlimited Championship trophy in hand, Hinton and the *Red Baron* crew were back to Mojave. The race had been moved to June 23 and 24, 1979.

Mac McClain rounds the pylons at Mojave '76 en route to the aircraft's first win with the Griffon engine. The Red Baron *crossed the finish line with a comfortable average speed of 406.718 mph. (Veronico Collection)*

The Red Baron *climbs out for the air start at Mojave 1976. (Veronico Collection)*

Hinton qualified at 404.815, and like the three races he had flown previously, the battle would be for second place. In the Unlimited Championship Race, Hinton dominated, finishing the race with an average speed of 396.181. Second place was taken by John Putman in P-51D *Ciuchetton* at 378.988 mph, followed by Clay Klabo in P-51D *Fat Cat* at 376.534 mph. Hinton was now four for four.

The team had its sights on the World Propeller Driven Speed Record, then held by Darryl Greenameyer and his Bearcat at 483.048 mph. Aerodynamicist Bruce Boland calculated that if the Griffon could produce 3,200 rpm at 110 inches of manifold pressure at a density altitude of 5,400 ft., the *Red Baron* would be able to fly 520 mph. "The team wanted to attempt the record in 1978, but, when fighting for a sponsor's money, the Mustang lost out to Greenameyer whose F-104 was also being sponsored by Browning," said Scoville. "As it wound up, Darryl got the course surveyed, and in 1978 he set the low altitude record for the jet. In August 1979, we were given the opportunity to set the record with the prop driven airplane. Browning had already paid to have the survey done, and we now had a rapport with the people at Photosonics who did the timing for Darryl. In a way it was better because we were able to iron out all the problems during Darryl's attempt. And when we went there, we didn't have any logistical problems as far as the course or the timing."

The team had a seven day sanction and battled weather problems that included wind one day, and rain the next. New speed records were actually set three times in four days. The first set of four passes, two north to south plus two south to north runs, averaged around 489 mph. "The second run we threw a rod out the side," Steve Hinton said. "We don't know why, but that was an engine that had twice lost its blower gears. Going from high power to idle, we think it might have stretched a rod bolt and then downstream later, it finally let go." The crew hurriedly

A day or two after this picture was taken, Darryl Greenameyer flew the Red Baron to an Unlimited Championship Race victory at an average speed of 430.703 mph. (William T. Larkins)

Notice the height of the tail, featuring an 18-inch cap, making it taller than a P-51H tail. The intake scoop over the top of the Griffon and the lack of the lower scoop as found on Merlin-powered Mustangs gave the Red Baron *a unique look. (William T. Larkins)*

changed the engine. Hinton got airborne for another attempt and set a record in the middle 490s. They were running out of weather and time. The Air Force wanted their training area back, and the team wanted one more try.

"It was the last day and the last time we had a chance to set the record," Hinton said. "It was a cold day, 65 degrees, and it was windy. They could hear me eight miles away that's how thick the air was. But we just had to go with it. We knew the plane would do it. Originally we went up there and knew it was capable of 515 or somewhere in that area and we did not set it over 500. We wanted to set it right around 500 so we could get a sponsor and come back and do it again. We weren't going out there to go as fast as we could. Had we had the right day, and we ran a little more power with it, yeah, we would have gone a lot faster. But at that time, that day, under that situation, that's the way it happened." The four-way pass averaged 499.018 mph. Hinton and the *Red Baron* were four for four, and now holders of the World Propeller Driven Speed Record.

From the deserts of Tonopah, the *Red Baron* team headed for Reno in September to turn the 9.8-mile course. This year, Mac McClain was flying the highly modified P-51 *Jeannie* (formerly *Miss Candace*). He set a new National and Reno qualifying-record speed of 446.93 mph. Hinton did too, posting an average speed of 441.90. John Crocker in *Sumthin' Else* was clocked at 432.71 mph. The competition was going to be tough.

In the first heat race, McClain edged Hinton out by seven-tenths of a second. In the second heat, Crocker's average speed was less than 3 mph faster than Hinton.

For the Unlimited Championship Race, the field saw the RB-51 compete against four other Mustangs flown by Crocker, McClain, Klabo, and Bill Harrison, a Sea Fury piloted by Lloyd Hamilton, and John Herlihy's Bearcat as an alternate starter. As the race began, McClain pulled out with a sick engine and Herlihy moved in to take his place. Harrison was out by the end of the second lap, having induction temperature problems. Herlihy was so far back, he pulled out after beginning the third lap. Crocker had pulled ahead of Hinton, and was widening his lead. Hinton kept putting power to

Miss R.J. Racing History

Year	Location	Pilot	Race	Place	Speed (mph)
1966	Reno	Chuck Hall	Consolation	Sixth	304.990
1967	Reno	Chuck Hall	Championship	Fourth	363.071
1968	Reno	Chuck Hall	Championship	Second	386.852
1969	Reno	Chuck Hall	Championship	Second	377.23
1970	Reno	Chuck Hall	Championship	did not qualify	
1970	Mojave	Chuck Hall	California 1,000	DNF lap 20	——

Roto-Finish Special Racing History

Year	Location	Pilot	Race	Place	Speed (mph)
1971	Reno	Gunther Balz	Championship	Fourth	412.101
1972	Reno	Gunther Balz	Championship	First	416.160
1973	Reno	John Wright	Championship	Third	407.495
1973	Mojave	Jack Sliker	California 1,000	Fourth	348.483

the engine, but it just wasn't running up to par. Pete Law said Hinton was pulling 115 inches of manifold pressure, but he wasn't getting any power because "one of the condensers in the mag was burned out and he was only firing on half the plugs. He kept going up and up in power, and it was all going in to making boost. None of it was going out the propeller."

While Crocker was taking the checkered flag at an average speed of 422.302 mph, things were beginning to turn ugly in the *Red Baron*. "It started running rough down the last straight away and, right as I made the last turn, it started shaking hard," Hinton said. "I pulled the throttle back and crossed the finish line climbing a little bit and then I pulled the throttle back and did a turn out. When I was turning back to the runway is when it quit cold. The supercharger gear drive burned up, which in itself isn't an end of story situation, but while getting the airplane back to the airport I lost all oil pressure, and the propellers went flat. The drag that the two propellers created is way more than anybody including myself imagined and it couldn't make the runway."

The supercharger gear drive controls the fuel pump, water pump, and the oil pump which in turn starved the prop governor of pressure. Oil pressure in the prop governor holds the pitch of the blades. Centrifugal twisting moment of the blades under the airloads forced the blades into flat pitch causing tremendous aerodynamic drag — it's just like putting the brakes on. With no possibility of making a runway, the *Red Baron* dropped into Lemon Valley.

All that could be seen from the pits and the bleachers was a fireball and black smoke. The wings had torn off

Red Baron Racing History

Year	Location	Pilot	Race	Place	Speed (mph)
1974	Reno	Roy McClain	Championship	DNF lap 1	——
1974	Mojave	Roy McClain	Championship	First	382.207
1975	Mojave	Roy McClain	Championship	DNF lap 2	——
1975	Reno	Roy McClain	Championship	Second	427.313
1976	Mojave	Roy McClain	Championship	First	406.718
1976	Reno	Roy McClain	Championship	DNF	——
1977	Reno	D. Greenameyer	Championship	First	430.703
1978	Reno	Steve Hinton	Championship	First	415.457
1978	Mojave	Steve Hinton	Championship	First	371.28
1979	Homestead	Steve Hinton	Championship	First	384.791
1979	Mojave	Steve Hinton	Championship	First	396.181
1979	Reno	Steve Hinton	Championship	Second	415.967

in the landing and Hinton rode the fuselage across the desert floor. Badly injured, he was airlifted to the hospital. After a month-long stay in the hospital, Hinton returned to aviation. Six years later he won the Unlimited Race, this time flying the R-4360 *Super Corsair*.

Hinton, reflecting on the *Red Baron* said, "It was a really great project. There was a lot of input from a lot of people. We had a great sponsor and it was a really exciting time — a lot of special moments. There were so many great people that made it really worth doing."

With the Reno home pylon in the background, the Red Baron *basks in the Nevada sun. Its wings have been painted white with the racer's name emblazoned across them.* (William T. Larkins)

Racer number "7," Strega, owned and piloted by Bill "Tiger" Destefani is a perennial champion. This highly-modified Mustang is powered by a Thorn-modified Rolls-Royce Merlin engine.
(A. Kevin Grantham)

In the early years at Reno, Miss America was owned and flown by Howie Keefe. At the 1971 races Keefe qualified third behind Balz and Shelton at 412.63 mph. The aircraft has passed through a number of owners and is still active in racing today. (Nicholas A. Veronico)

The Sanders brothers' Pratt & Whitney R-4360-powered Hawker Sea Fury is one of the most powerful unlimited racers to compete in the Gold Race. It can easily post 450 mph laps without really stressing its engine. (A. Kevin Grantham)

Lloyd Hamilton's Baby Gorilla *made its first Reno racing appearance in 1972. Hamilton qualified the ex-Royal Navy Bristol Centarus-powered Sea Fury at 372.55 mph. Hamilton was an outstanding competitor and gave Gunther Balz a run for his money in the Heat races at Reno 1972. (Nicholas A. Veronico)*

By 1971, Lyle Shelton had repainted his Bearcat into a white and purple scheme and renamed the plane Phoenix I. *Gunther Balz qualified the Roto-Finish Special at 419.50 mph with Shelton a close second at 418.01 mph. In the 1971 Unlimited Championship race, both Shelton and Balz finished behind Darryl Greenameyer's Bearcat* Conquest I. *(Armand Veronico Collection)*

Reno 1978 had some of the harshest race weather ever. On Sunday, it rained, snowed, and the wind howled. The clouds cleared enough for Don Whittington and Steve Hinton to battle it out during the Unlimited Championship Race. Hinton took the checkered flag at an average speed of 415.457 mph. (William T. Larkins)

Returning to Reno in 1979, the racer wears the colors of its new sponsor — Michelob Light. Steve Hinton would finish the Unlimited Championship Race with a sick Griffon in second place at an average speed of 415.967 mph. (William T. Larkins)

The shattered Griffon lays on the floor of Lemon Valley. Seeing the amount of damage done, it is hard to imagine that Steve Hinton was able to survive the crash. Six years later, Hinton won the Unlimited Race in the Super Corsair. (Grantham Collection)

When the wings separated from the fuselage in the crash, they burst into flame and scorched the surrounding desert floor. Hinton, still strapped into his seat, continued to ride the fuselage to a stop. The remains of the wing and main gear show the extent of the damage done to the racer. (Grantham Collection)

The twisted tail of the Red Baron is the only recognizable piece of the racer. This section split at the rear of the oil cooler exhaust door. (Grantham Collection)

Steve Hinton listens to the prerace briefing. Hinton would survive the crash of the Red Baron *and return to win the Reno Gold again in 1985 flying the R-4360-powered* Super Corsair. *(Nicholas A. Veronico)*

Note the extended wing/fuselage faring in this side view. Small writing next to the Champion spark plug logo reads: Owner: Ed Browning; underneath, Engineers — Bruce Boland, Pete Law. On the wing tip: Crew Chief Randy Scoville. Under the PPG Paint logo it reads: Insured by — Frank B. Hall, Agent — Don Bingham. (William T. Larkins)

WOR3LD JET

The Reno Air Race Association celebrated its 25th anniversary in 1988 with 35 entries in the unlimited air racing class. Included in this record turnout were three aircraft new to the sport: a highly-modified Yak 11, *Mr. Awesome*; John Dilley's novice racer *Vendetta* combined a set of Lear Jet 23 wings with a Mustang fuselage; and Don and Bill Whittington's Griffon-powered contra-rotating propeller driven P-51D, *World Jet*.

The idea of building a Griffon-powered Mustang was spawned nearly nine months before the 1988 Reno air races. A large undertaking with precious little time, the Whittingtons had already acquired a cache of surplus Griffon motors and parts from the *Miss Budweiser* boat racing team that had recently converted to turbine engines. The Whittingtons then began work on fitting a Mk. 74 Griffon to a stock Mustang. The alterations made to the P-51D airframe were similar in scope to what had previously occurred with the RB-51 *Red Baron*. A more streamlined, cut-down canopy was made to fit the craft, and the shorter D-model tail was replaced with a larger P-51H type vertical stabilizer. As was learned with the *Red Baron*, the Griffon power arrangement tends to make a Mustang fly sideways, so a tail with more vertical surface area is needed for better directional control and stability. The installation of the Griffon Mk. 74 was achieved with a new mount and a very slick cowling, topped with small air intake for the PR100 carburetor. By September the task of building the *World Jet*

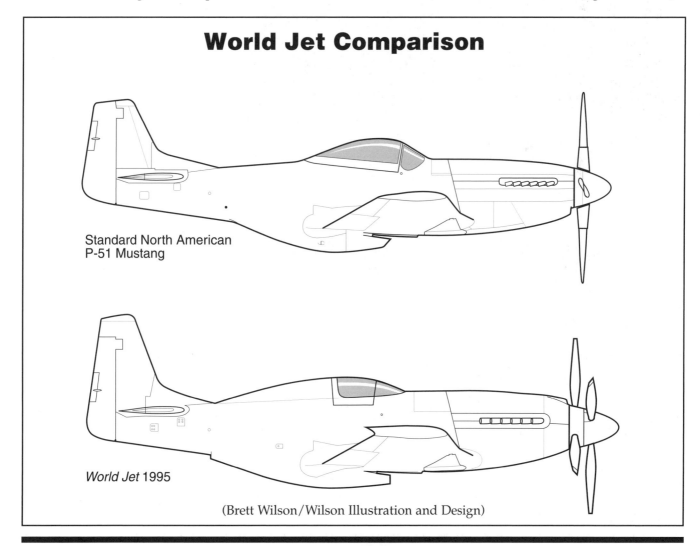

World Jet Comparison

Standard North American
P-51 Mustang

World Jet 1995

(Brett Wilson/Wilson Illustration and Design)

When World Jet *appeared at the 35th annual Reno National Championship Air Races in 1988, the sight of counter-rotating propellers caused quite a commotion.* (Nicholas A. Veronico)

racer was somehow completed in time to enter the 1988 Reno National Championship Air Races.

The qualifying rounds in 1988 were exciting times, with Lyle Shelton's *Rare Bear* posting a record-breaking speed of 474.622 mph. Steve Hinton, piloting the home-built racer, *Tsunami*, was close behind Shelton at 470.899 mph. Don Whittington coaxed 453.078 mph out of *World Jet*, which was good enough to capture the fifth highest qualifying speed of the event. However, engine problems soon developed and the plane

was grounded for repairs for a short period of time. Then a propeller governor malfunctioned and this troublesome device would continue to plague the *World Jet* racing team throughout the rest of the competition. (Reportedly, the propeller control seemed to work fine as long as the blade rotation was kept under 3,000 revolutions per minute. However, it would tend to runaway at higher RPMs.)

On Sunday, Bob Hoover's yellow P-51D paced nine racing machines above Stead Field as they prepared for the quest of the elusive Gold Trophy. Shortly after Hoover started the race, Don Whittington sounded the familiar "Mayday" distress call over the radio as he pulled the silver race number 09 up and off the course.

"Just as Hoover called, 'Gentlemen, you have a race,' I pushed it up a little more, I was adding power," Whittington said. "Just at that point, he (Hoover) had already pulled up, and we were coming upon the interstate, that's when it happened!"

The propeller governor could not pump sufficient pressure to keep the blades at the pitch setting Whittington had called for, "and the blades went the other direction. The RPMs went to 5,500 or 6,000 and blew the spinner apart," Whittington related after the race.

"My first thought was that I was going to have to get out because it was shaking rather badly. I started to do that, but that wouldn't work because I realized I was going too slow. I had already slowed down to roughly 130 mph indicated. I looked down and I could see I was over a populated area, so I pushed everything back up, and it didn't shake any worse. I went ahead and turned

the mag switch back on and it fired. I gave it a little throttle to get a little airspeed going forward, because it was coming down — I mean it was coming straight down!"

Whittington bellied the Mustang onto the Lemon Valley dry lakebed, east of Stead Field. Fortunately, Don Whittington was able to walk away from the successful wheels-up landing, but *World Jet* would be off the racing circuit for six years while the damage was repaired.

March 25 and 26, 1995, saw the first post-belly landing appearance of *World Jet* at the second Phoenix 500 Air Races. Don Whittington qualified the Griffon-powered racer, now carrying race number 38, in sixth position at 373.379 mph. Each race would be five laps of a 7.2-mile course — nearly two miles shorter,

and much tighter than Reno's 9-mile course. In Heat 1A on Saturday, March 25, Whittington did not start. Although he took off and formed-up for the race, he could not get his landing gear to fully retract. Whittington elected to land and solve the gear problem as there was still a full weekend of racing ahead, although his failure to finish in Heat 1A dropped him down into Sunday's Silver race.

The field for the Unlimited Silver race consisted of three P-51s — Jimmy Leeward's *Cloud Dancer*, Brent Hisey's *Miss America*, and Whittington — Tom Camp's Yak-11; Nelson Ezell's Hawker Fury; and Howard Pardue's F8F-1 Bearcat. The first lap began with Pardue leading Ezell, Whittington, Hisey, Camp, and Leeward. At the start of the second lap, Whittington passed

Ezell and had Pardue in his sights. Near the end of the second lap, *World Jet* passed the Bearcat, and Whittington never looked back. When the checkered flag fell, Whittington had won the race with an average speed of 381.745 mph. Having such a commanding lead, the races were actually behind Whittington in the battles for second and third and fourth and fifth — Pardue came in second at 365.524 mph followed by Ezell at 364.929 mph, and finishing fourth was Camp at 314.233 with Hisey on his heels at 313.043. As the winner of the Silver race, Whittington had the opportunity to move up into the Gold race, which he did, surrendering his Silver first place prize money.

The competition in the Gold Race was more of Whittington's caliber — four P-51s including Bill "Tiger"

Don Whittington taxies out for the 1989 Unlimited Gold Race. Many of the lessons learned on the Red Baron *were incorporated into Whittington's racer.* (Nicholas A. Veronico)

Destefani flying *Strega* (with a stock engine after blowing its racing engine), Bill "Rhino" Rheinschild in *Risky Business*, Delbert Williams in *Voodoo Chile*, and Whittington; John Penny in the highly modified F8F-2 *Rare Bear*; and two Sea Furies — Dennis Sanders in *Dreadnought* and Brian Sanders in *Fury*. Down the chute and into the first lap, *World Jet* was in the lead, followed by *Strega* and *Rare Bear*. Near the end of the second lap, Penney, at the controls of the Bearcat, pulled away from the pack, leading the race until the end. *Risky Business* pulled out in the second lap, followed by *Voodoo Chile* in the third. *Rare Bear* finished the race with an average speed of 443.372 mph, followed by *Dreadnought* at

426.056 mph, *Strega* at 409.039, Whittington and *World Jet* at 386.759 mph, and *Fury* at 374.352 mph.

Six months later it was time for the running of September's Champions in Reno, Nevada. *World Jet* and her crew arrived ready to race, and ready to win. *World Jet* qualified at a respectable 380.951 mph. On Wednesday, prior to the official start of the heat races, bolts in the Griffon engine's nose case sheared. The crew worked through the afternoon and evening, and the plane was ready the next morning. On a test flight early Thursday morning, a coolant line broke spraying the interior of the canopy obstructing Whittington's forward vision. He jetti-

soned the low profile canopy and brought the plane back to Stead for an uneventful landing. The canopy was recovered, the line repaired, and *World Jet* was ready to race again that afternoon. During the last heat race on Thursday, *World Jet* blew a coolant pop-off valve, scalding Don Whittington. After declaring a "Mayday," Whittington landed safely. While he received treatment for minor burns, the crew set about repairing the racer. In Friday's first race, Whittington again suffered minor cooling problems, but went on to win the heat with an average speed of 356.555 mph. During Saturday's heat race, *World Jet* finished fourth at an average speed of 343.934 mph.

A sorry end to an exciting year. Don Whittington successfully belly-landed World Jet *as the Unlimited Gold racers were coming down the chute.* World Jet's *prop governor failed and, reminiscent of the* Red Baron, *the prop blade went into flat pitch forming a giant air brake. The aircraft was trucked to Whittington's Ft. Lauderdale, Florida, home base and rebuilt.* (Nicholas A. Veronico)

World Jet Championship Racing Career

Year	Venue	Race	Place	Speed
1988	Reno, Nevada	Qualifying	——	453.078 mph
1988	Reno, Nevada	Unlimited Gold	DNF	——
1995	Phoenix, Arizona	Qualifying	——	373.379 mph
1995	Phoenix, Arizona	Unlimited Silver	First	381.745 mph
1995	Phoenix, Arizona	Unlimited Gold	Fourth	386.759 mph
1995	Reno, Nevada	Qualifying	——	380.951 mph
1995	Reno, Nevada	Unlimited Silver	First	379.491 mph
1995	Reno, Nevada	Unlimited Gold	Sixth	390.456 mph

For Sunday's Unlimited Silver Race, Whittington and *World Jet* would do battle with four Mustangs, Howard Pardue's Bearcat, and Tom Camp's Yak-11. From the start Whittington ruled the race course, finishing with an average speed of 379.491 mph, far ahead of second-place finisher Howard Pardue. Upon landing, Whittington forfeited his Silver Race purse money thereby allowing him to move up to the Unlimited Gold Race. By moving up, Whittington would now compete against eight other racers — the toughest competition in the class. David Price in *Dago Red*, "Tiger" Destefani in *Strega*, and John Penney in *Rare Bear*, were the odds-on favorites to win. The field was rounded out by Howard Pardue in his *Sea Fury*, Bob Hannah in the P-51 *Voodoo Chile*, Whittington in *World Jet*, Brian Sanders in *Fury*, and Stu Eberhardt in *Merlin's Magic*. The race finished with *Strega* taking the checkered flag at 467.029 mph, followed by *Rare Bear* at 465.159 mph, and *Dago Red* at 449.137 mph. Having been lapped by the three lead airplanes, *World Jet* finished sixth at 390.456 mph, nearly 80 mph slower than the winner.

Although the aircraft had the potential, *World Jet* never realized an Unlimited Gold Race finish above fourth place. The Whittington brothers retired *World Jet* from racing and it is reported that the aircraft is being returned to stock configuration.

World Jet *returned to race on the Unlimited circuit in 1995. Crew members button-up the racer in preparation for a heat race.* (Betty S. Anderson)

At Reno '95, Whittington taxies World Jet *for takeoff. Whittington qualified the Griffon-powered racer at 380.951 mph. Certainly an acceptable qualifying speed, but not a Gold Race winning performance. The racer was plagued with mechanical troubles the entire race week.* (Nicholas A. Veronico)

Ready to race: World Jet *looks fantastic all buttoned-up on the Reno ramp. During Saturday's heat race, Whittington had to contend with cooling problems and only turned in a fourth place finish at an average speed of 343.934 mph.* (Jim Dunn)

Above and Below: *In 1995,* World Jet *wore a polished metal finish with neon green wings and a waving American flag on both sides of the fuselage. Many pilots believe* World Jet's *upward hinging canopy could cause problems when attempting to rescue a pilot in the event of an off-field landing where the aircraft came to rest inverted.* (Nicholas A. Veronico)

Detail shot of the canopy area showing the cut-down windscreen, built-up turtle deck, and the modified wing tips.
(Nicholas A. Veronico)

Above and Below: *The pit crew attends to last-minute details as the Griffon comes to life. As the propellers swing in opposite directions, the visual effect is mesmerizing.* (Tim Weinschenker)

Unlike the Red Baron *and later* Miss Ashley II, World Jet's *cockpit turtle deck curves down to meet the tail fillet.* (Tim Weinschenker)

Nose cowling detail in the Phoenix pit area. (Tim Weinschenker)

RACEPLANE TECH
S E R I E S

Above and below: *Extensive wing faring and turtle deck modifications are evident in this Phoenix '95 view of* World Jet *in the Unlimited pits. This aircraft also sported a more conventional P-51D type vertical stabilizer.* (Tim Weinschenker)

With the prop off, Whittington's crew replaces a number of sheared bolts in the nose case at Reno '95. (Tim Weinschenker)

RACEPLANE **TECH**
S E R I E S

At Phoenix, World Jet *wore its racing number in a neon green circle on its tail.* (Jim Dunn)

The props are reinstalled and some last-minute fine tuning is done to the Griffon engine. (Tim Weinschenker)

The rear prop goes back on in time to race on Wednesday, September 13, at Reno '95. In the true competitive spirit, many rival racing teams will lend parts, tools, and even mechanics to help a fellow racer get back into the air. (Tim Weinschenker)

Moving the racer to the fueling area before the afternoon heat race gives spectators an unobstructed view of this unique aircraft. (Nicholas A. Veronico)

RACEPLANE **TECH**
S E R I E S

Compare the racer's markings, above at Reno '88 to its later colors at Reno '95 (below). (Above: Paul Neuman; Below: A. Kevin Grantham)

In 1988, John Dilley, of Fort Wayne, Indiana, arrived at the Reno Air Races with a radical looking P-51 with Lear Jet wings. "Our concept when we started was, keep everything just as simple, simple, simple as possible," said Dilley. "We wanted a light-weight, high-speed operation." To achieve these goals, Dilley first replaced the slower thicker Mustang wing with a more modern air foil that is rated to fly at speeds in excess of 500 mph. Then methods were used to reduce drag and to lighten the airplane as much as possible. Dilley decided to also employ an intake duct that had been developed by the National Advisory Committee for Aeronautics (NACA) during the late 1940s. The design and measurements for the NACA duct, as Dilley put it, "believe it or not were taken from an article that appeared in *Popular Mechanics* magazine. The finished duct had two times better recovery than the intake used on a stock Mustang. The reason it was so effective is because we designed — maybe by accident, or whatever — the NACA duct with the proper degree in the floor, which is very critical. The NACA can become basically useless if its floor angle is off by a degree or so."

VENDETTA
Mfg. By: North American Dilley, Inc.
Model Number: P-51R
Top Speed: 530 mph
Features: Lear 23 Wing
Lear Horizontal Stabilizer

Vendetta in flight shortly after its completion. (John Dilley, circa 1988)

Landing gear is another area where Dilley looked to reduce weight. "I wanted to come up with something that was basically the same length as the Mustang," recalled Dilley. "I started to look around and found the Piper Aerostar gear, which is very light. I took the upper half of the Aerostar and converted that to an air-over-oil because the Aerostar originally had two fillers so I converted it to one. I changed the snubbing system inside to give a bit more snubbing because the Aerostar gear didn't pass its initial drop test according to the original designer. (We were able to reach the original designer and builder of the Aerostar landing gear. This allowed us to acquire some original materials and to apply some analysis to make sure our strengths were where they should be.) Then we took a Piper Cheyenne lower fork that we machined to the fit. We also used a

(Bill Rogers Collection, circa 1988)

Cessna 400 series actuator that has a mechanical lock. The only way you can unlock it is with pressure. We then used sequencing valves from a Mustang and also from the Cessna system."

It took Dilly three years and over $800,000 to produce the racer that he named *Vendetta*. In the end, the plane was 1,000 pounds lighter than a stock Mustang and had an expected top speed of 525 mph.

Unfortunately, engine problems plagued *Vendetta* throughout its very short career. Dilley, on a less than perfect running Merlin, managed to post a qualifying speed of just over 300 mph. In the end, the sick engine kept him from competing in any of the 1988 heat races. However, he did manage to prove his design concept. "The aircraft actually did reach a 530 mph speed that was clocked by radar at 5,000 feet in a continuous three 'G' turn over the nine-mile racecourse," said Dilley. Then a few weeks after the races, *Vendetta* experienced another engine failure that forced Dilley to make a wheels-up landing in a field, which resulted in considerable damage to the aircraft. The price tag for repairing the damage was in the hundreds of thousands of dollars, so Dilley decided to retire racer #19 and used the stock P-51 parts on another Mustang.

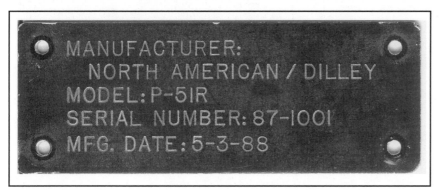

MANUFACTURER:
    NORTH AMERICAN / DILLEY
MODEL: P-5IR
SERIAL NUMBER: 87-1001
MFG. DATE: 5-3-88

Data plate of the newly-built Vendetta. (Bill Rogers Collection, circa 1999)

After two first-place finishes in the Unlimited Silver and a fourth in the Unlimited Gold, the Whittingtons decided to retire World Jet *and convert it back to a stock P-51D.* (Tim Weinschenker)

After the introductions, World Jet's *Griffon comes to life, ready to race.* (Bill Rogers)

COLORFUL RACERS

The sport of air racing features paint schemes that show off the sleek lines of each racer. In fact, these schemes help build a strong following of loyal fans who cheer for their favorite aircraft and race pilot as the racer rounds the pylons. Whether the plane and pilot are consistent winners, world speed record holders, or perpetual underdogs, these have no bearing when air racing enthusiasts speak of their favorite race team — each is a winner for simply competing.

Although only three Griffon-powered P-51s have turned the pylons to date, each aircraft has had a distinct look and livery. This color section features the *Red Baron*, *World Jet*, and a detailed look at the innovative modifications made to *Miss Ashley II*'s carburetor and radiator inlet scoops. Appropriately, the color section opens with the *Red Baron*, the innovator in the marriage of Mustang airframe and Griffon powerplant. The technological lessons learned by the *Red Baron* team were further expanded upon by the Whittington brothers' *World Jet* and by the Gary Levitz/Bill Rogers team's *Miss Ashley II*. Photos on the following pages allow for a comparison of the engine installation and downdraft carburetor intakes as well as the canopy configurations of *Miss Ashley II* and *World Jet*.

Detail shot of the Red Baron's *counter-rotating propellers and belly scoop. The highly modified Mustang has just arrived at Sacramento, California's McClellan Air Force Base open house on September 8, 1979. McClellan was an en route stop on the way to Stead Field.*
(Jim Dunn)

Having recently set the record for the World's Fastest Propeller Driven aircraft at 499.010 mph, the public was eager to catch a glimpse of the racer. The record was formerly held by Darryl Greenameyer and his modified F8F Bearcat at 483.048 mph.
(Jim Dunn)

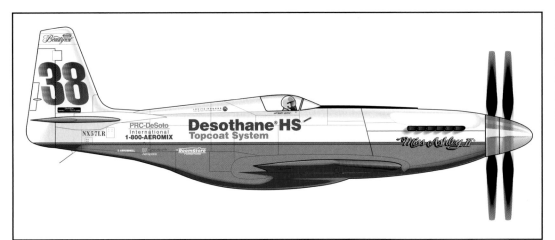

Profile of Miss Ashley II *in the aircraft's final configuration with modified belly scoop.* (Brett Wilson)

Bill Rogers and pilot Gary Levitz in 1998. Miss Ashley II's *canopy configuration gave the racer the streamlined profile while offering the pilot comparatively good forward vision. It was also designed so the pilot could easily slide it back in emergency situations.* (A. Kevin Grantham)

The Griffon's engine mount, which was constructed from 2.5-inch tubular steel pipe, perfectly cradled the 2,240 cubic inch engine. The small cylinder with white ends that is shown attached to the engine mount is lead ballast that is added to the front of the aircraft to counterbalance the weight of the nitrous oxide tanks which were installed behind the pilot's seat. (Nicholas A. Veronico)

John Dilley was one of the first to effectively employ a NACA Duct on an unlimited racer. He found that many of the design dimensions of the NACA Duct are very critical. In the end, his NACA variant air worked very well on his racer Vendetta. By contrast, the effort to adapt a similar design on John Sandberg's purpose-built racer Tsunami proved to be less than successful in delivering the needed ram air to the throat of the Merlin's downdraft carburetor, so a more conventional type intake was used. The Levitz/Rogers team was the latest in the series to try and adopt the NACA technology. Dick Aley, one of the team's engineers, studied government test reports and designed an intake that was very true to the original NACA design. Aley felt that the lower placement of the carburetor on the Griffon engine also aided Miss Ashley's ram air performance by giving the air flow more time to recover after it made its downward 90-degree turn. In effect, the smooth transition allowed a greater volume of air to flow to the carburetor with less resistance. (Brett Wilson)

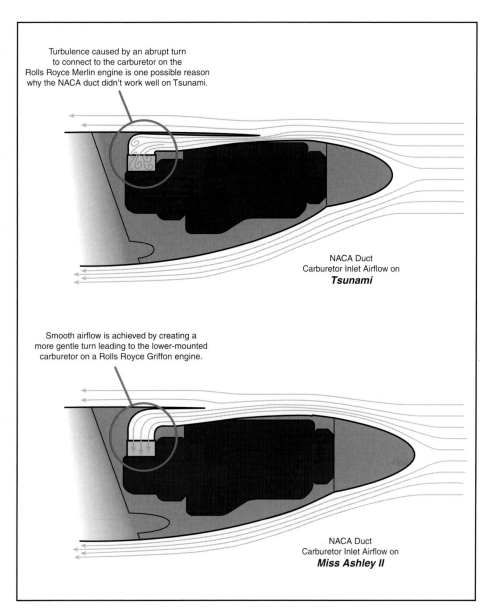

Turbulence caused by an abrupt turn to connect to the carburetor on the Rolls Royce Merlin engine is one possible reason why the NACA duct didn't work well on Tsunami.

NACA Duct
Carburetor Inlet Airflow on
Tsunami

Smooth airflow is achieved by creating a more gentle turn leading to the lower-mounted carburetor on a Rolls Royce Griffon engine.

NACA Duct
Carburetor Inlet Airflow on
Miss Ashley II

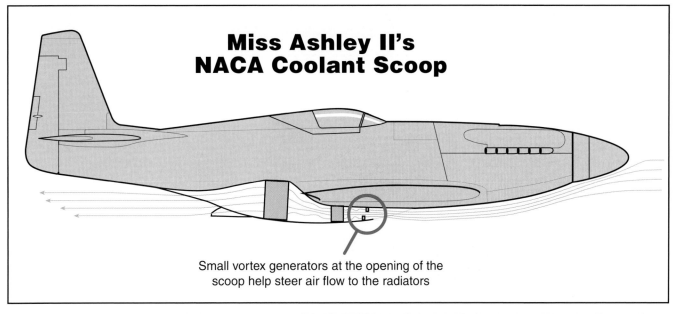

Miss Ashley II's
NACA Coolant Scoop

Small vortex generators at the opening of the scoop help steer air flow to the radiators

World Jet rounds the pylons at Phoenix '95 to finish in first place in the Silver Race at an average speed of 381.745 mph. Whittington elected to forego his Silver Race win in order to move up to the Gold Race.
(Jim Dunn)

World Jet is towed in front of the grandstands for the introduction of the Unlimited Gold competitors.
(A. Kevin Grantham)

Running up the Griffon at Phoenix '95. This view shows how far back the Griffon sits on the Mustang fuselage.
(Scott E. Germain)

MISS A4SHLEY II

Miss *Ashley II* made her debut at the 34th annual Reno National Championship Air Races in 1997, but the genesis of this fine looking racing machine really began 27 years earlier.

The year was 1970 when a young Bill Rogers and a high school friend made their way from Texas to Reno, Nevada, for the National Championship Air Races. Although Bill had never attended an air race before, he was not exactly a novice because he had already read almost everything that had been printed about the sport. He also grew up with the stories told by his father with regard to the post World War II races that included tales about the highly-modified, emerald green North American P-51 racer known as *Beguine*. Suffice it to say, Bill had the racing bug long before he arrived at the Reno Airport. The actual racing events are held at Stead Field, formerly Stead Air Force Base, which is located approximately 10 miles north of Reno. A long walk for a couple of boys who weren't old enough to rent a car. But they finally got there to witness the speed and power of "the fastest motor sport in the world."

Not content to be just a spectator, Rogers soon found himself crewing for Gary Levitz who was actively racing a Lockheed P-38 Lightning during the early 1970s. In later years, Rogers also crewed for Alan Preston, Bill Rheinschild, and worked on racing airplanes with names like *Precious Metal, Risky Business,* and *Dago Red.* Along the way,

he gathered the knowledge and experience that he would one day need to build his dream racer. In 1988, Rogers took the first steps toward his dream when he purchased the salvaged wreckage of the *Red Baron.* For the next few years Rogers collected components while he laid out the basic look of his racer. His original hybrid design resembled a Rolls-Royce Griffon-powered Supermarine Mk.XIV Spitfire with a cut-down canopy and a North American P-51H vertical tail. However, these design ideas would take on a much different scheme after talking to John Dilley.

"I was looking for Mustang parts when I first talked to John Dilley in 1991," said Rogers. "During our discussion we talked about — you know, air racing stuff — but eventually we got around to talking about

Vendetta (see pages 63/64). John planted the notion in my head that his original idea of mating a faster Lear Jet wing to a Mustang might be the way to go. I was going to have to find or build a wing anyway so, I decided to further pursue this concept. Sometime later, while on a business trip to Fort Wayne, Indiana, I met Dilley for dinner, and we talked some more. The following week I purchased a damaged Lear 23 wing, tail, landing gear, and racing canopy."

The years after Reno 1991 were a busy time for Bill Rogers. Not only was he heavily involved in getting the plans for his racer together, he was also spending a great deal of so-called "temporary duty" in Seattle, Washington, for his employer, Southwest Airlines. While away on travel Rogers began the construction

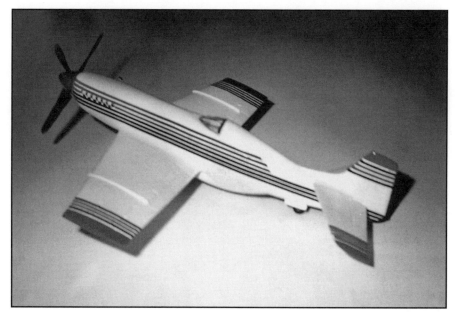

This wooden model reflects Bill Rogers initial Vendetta II *racer concept.* (Bill Rogers Collection, circa 1992)

Miss Ashley II Evolution

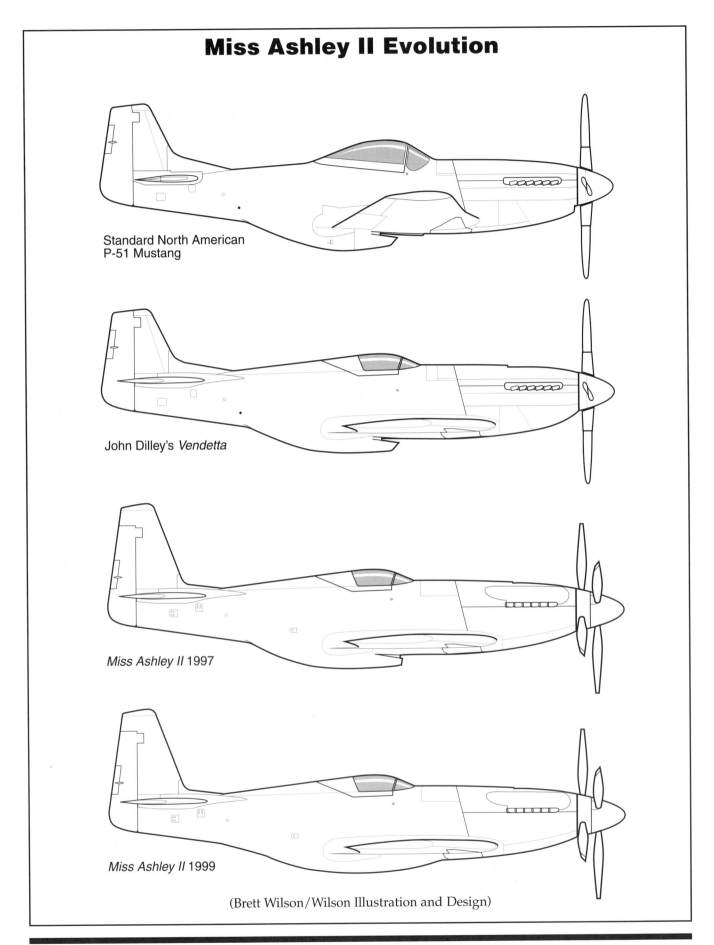

Standard North American
P-51 Mustang

John Dilley's *Vendetta*

Miss Ashley II 1997

Miss Ashley II 1999

(Brett Wilson/Wilson Illustration and Design)

The Lear 23 main wing that Rogers purchased from John Dilley required a great deal of attention before it was airworthy again. (Bill Rogers Collection, circa 1992)

of a wooden model, and it was from this archetype that the design validation of his future racing airplane began to take shape.

At about the same time, Rogers obtained P-51 production drawings from the National Air & Space Museum in Washington, D.C., as well as purchasing some equipment from the now defunct Braniff Airlines. He also enlisted his younger brother, Terry, who would help with the construction of a scratch-built Mustang fuselage. (Now, it might possibly have been easier for most to go out and acquire a suitable North American-built fuselage. However, Bill Rogers has a keen sense of warbird history, and he really didn't want to be party to using scarce parts that could better be used in an authentic Mustang restoration.) Progress was slow but steady for a

couple of years, and Rogers continued to commute back to Texas on weekends in order to keep the project alive. The stress of being in one place while your heart is really in another finally paid off when the Rogers' scratch-built P-51 fuselage was completed. The basic unit was built per the North American Aviation drawings with the exception of moving the cockpit section aft and modifying it to accept the *Vendetta* racing canopy.

Bill Rogers' job as a Southwest Airlines Tech Rep was permanently transferred from Dallas, Texas, to Everett, Washington, in September 1993. Rogers then decided that it would be best to move the project to nearby Arlington Municipal Airport, rather than to continue the taxing commute to Texas each weekend. After the move, work contin-

ued on the fuselage, wing, and tail cone jig. Although, a monumental amount of work had already been accomplished, it was becoming apparent to Rogers that he was going to need additional help to complete the project.

In 1994, the rumors of Bill Rogers' new, purpose-built air racer had made their way to Reno. Coincidentally, his old friend Gary Levitz appeared to be interested in sponsoring a warbird project. Levitz was leaning toward putting some money into the restoration of the Confederate Air Force's ill-fated P-82 Twin Mustang. (Warbird enthusiasts might recall that the CAF P-82 was damaged some years back when the main gear collapsed while taxiing. Also, one might remember that Gary Levitz was one of the few CAF pilots who really knew how to han-

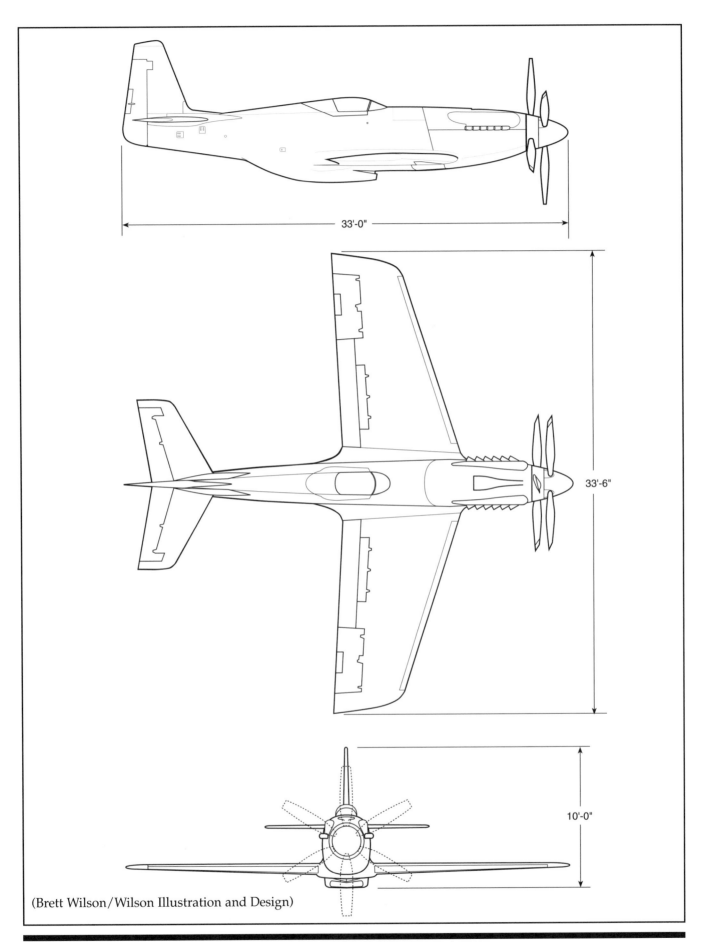

33'-0"

33'-6"

10'-0"

(Brett Wilson/Wilson Illustration and Design)

dle the big North American fighter.) Levitz took a look at the racing project and was very impressed. In early 1995, Levitz changed his mind about the P-82 and, subsequently, the two friends formed a partnership under the name of Levitz/Rogers Air Race Development, Inc. In February of the same year, the project was moved to Hangar 38, which also happens to be Gary Levitz' racing number, at Paine Field, Everett, Washington.

The influx of new capital helped Rogers focus on acquiring a proper racing engine such as the Rolls-Royce Griffon. (In previous years the *Red Baron* racing team had proven the Griffon's suitability for the sport by setting a new world-speed record for a piston-powered aircraft, of 499.018 mph in 1979, and by capturing four first-place wins between 1976 and 1979.) Rogers was able to secure five surplus Avro Shackleton Griffon Mk. 58 engines that he had located in England. Apparently, Rolls-Royce had sold these surplus engines to various individuals shortly after the Royal Air Force retired its last Shackleton patrol bomber in 1991. Rogers' search led him to one fellow who was going to install the 2,200 cubic inch engine in a car. Another owner had ideas of installing his Griffon in a boat. As luck would have it, neither of these projects ever came to fruition, and Rogers was fortunate enough to not only corner the English Rolls-Royce Griffon market but was also successful in acquiring five complete three-blade propellers and a large cache of spare parts.

The typical Griffon Mk. 58 engine comes equipped with a Standard English updraft fuel-injection system. However, the Levitz/Rogers team wanted to use a similar engine

carburetor setup as was used on *Red Baron*, so certain modifications would have to be made in order to accomplish this marriage. Team member Bob Manelski explains: "We used a PR58 downdraft carburetor that was originally used on a DC-6.

In order to use the PR58, we modified what was affectionately referred to as the 'horses ass' (this is the piece that adapts the carb to the blower). It's called that due to its visual likeness to the same before modification. What we did was unbolt the

The wing tips used on Miss Ashley II *were modeled after the type used on the Boeing/USAF EC-135 aircraft.* (Bill Rogers Collection, circa 1996)

Interior of the Lear 23 main wing offered ample room for fuel and water tanks. (Bill Rogers Collection, circa 1992)

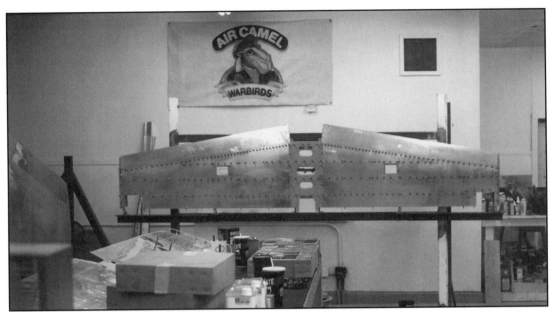

stock unit from the blower inlet, mill off the mounting flange, and weld on a plate which inverts the bolt pattern where it attaches to the blower. The carburetor end is also milled off and a PR58 mounting flange welded on. We also added a flange that was drilled and tapped out for the water-injection (ADI) port. The PR58 pressure carburetor functions as a metering unit that measures the airflow and pressure and supplies fuel to the original Griffon fuel-discharge nozzle for delivery to the engine."

The wing and the fuselage were finally mated in early 1996. "I was really surprised when the mounting locations on the wing and fuselage came together without any adjustment whatsoever," said Rogers. The hybrid Frankenstein-type landing gear, composed of Piper Aerostar uppers, Piper Cheyenne lowers, Cessna 421 retractable struts, Cessna Caravan wheel assemblies, and Gulfstream nose tires, used in the main wing was the same that had been used on John Dilley's *Vendetta*. The mounting of the big Griffon followed shortly thereafter. Again, Rogers could have possibly gone out and found a suitable surplus Griffon

engine mount but instead decided to use a stronger approach to mating the engine to the airframe.

Team member and master builder Gordon Cole flew out to Everett. He took some measurements, built a mockup out of exhaust pipes, and then delivered a two and one-half inch tubular steel engine mount that not only had the perfect fit, but was strong enough to possibly support the weight of a Patton tank. Meanwhile, Rogers contacted Unlimited Airframes of London, England, and requested a Spitfire cowling that would fit a Mustang firewall on one end and a Shackleton spinner on the other. The English company was a bit apprehensive at first, but soon delivered a cowling fabricated from drawings supplied by Bill Rogers. The cowling required a little custom fitting, but the addition was the touch the Levitz/Rogers "Learstang" — as some called it — needed to make it look like a racing plane.

With most of the major components completed, it was time to start installing the internal workings of the new racer. Project engineer Dick Aley ran center of gravity (CG) cal-

culations based on the measured weight of the aircraft. "I would ask Bill to have the plane weighed every time a major component was installed," said Aley. "The goal was to try and keep the CG between 23 and 27 percent of the mean aerodynamic cord (MAC)." This attention to detail and empirical approach of frequently checking the airplane's CG paid off by eventually producing a near perfectly-balanced racer. Sometimes components that seemed to be too heavy from a paper design standpoint turned out to fit the project very well. Bob Manelski recalls, "One of my first projects on the racer was the design and fabrication of the tail wheel unlock mechanism. Because of my day job at Boeing, I was used to making everything as light as possible. I remember talking with Bill about an idea I had that I thought was good, but too heavy. We ended up using it because at the time we had just weighed the airplane and it needed aft CG."

By mid-summer 1996 it appeared that the Levitz/Rogers racer had a slim chance of making it to the Reno Air Races in September. However, it was not to be. There's a great deal

The jig needed to fabricate the scratch-built fuselage was constructed by Gordon Cole. Bill Rogers' brother Terry worked on the project until it was moved to Washington. (Bill Rogers Collection, circa 1993)

Rogers purchased his first two Griffon engines from John Seevers in 1990. (Bill Rogers Collection, circa 1990)

View of Miss Ashley II, *complete with engine and vertical tail. The rudder assembly was patterned from the original P-51H rudder, salvaged from Don Whittington's P-51* Precious Metal. Precious Metal *was lost in a crash into the Gulf of Mexico off the coast of Texas in 1990.* (Rogers Collection, circa 1996)

involved in constructing a scratch-built airplane, and time ran out on getting the airplane to the races. "I can tell you that having both the North American and Dilley drawings was a plus, but you can't build a complete airplane from the drawings alone," said Rogers. "There have been a number of times when we have stopped work and wondered, 'Now how did John do that?' Fortunately, Dilley gave me a great number of photos that he had taken during various stages of the *Vendetta's* construction, and they helped a

great deal. In fact, we would not have been to able do what we have done without them."

Missing the races was disappointing but at the same time a blessing in disguise for the Levitz/Rogers racing organization because it allowed more time to work on the airplane. In the off-season, they fine-tuned the engine and every system was checked and rechecked. Bill Rogers also was very fortunate to attract Courtaulds Aerospace, (now PRC Desoto International) a technology leader in the manu-

facture of sealants and coatings for the aviation industry, and BF Goodrich as major sponsors.

In May 1997, the U.S. Federal Aviation Administration (FAA) certified the Levitz/Rogers racer as an "amateur built experimental." On June 6, 1997, renowned test pilot Skip Holm flew the unpainted airplane on its first flight. Holm reported a few minor items that needed some attention, but for the most part commented on how well the aircraft flew. More flight-testing followed and the plane made its first public appearance at a small Experimental Aircraft Association (EAA) gathering at Arlington Airport. Holm was again at the controls and he, at the request of the FAA, put on a fantastic low-level flight demonstration. Unfortunately, a landing gear door departed the plane during the flight. It turned out that the AT-6 gear door fitting was not strong enough to cope with the stress associated with high speeds, so the door fittings were redesigned and strengthened. Later in the summer, sponsor B.F. Goodrich, using paint that was supplied by the team's primary sponsor, Courtaulds Aerospace, painted the Levitz/Rogers racer.

Miss Ashley's *final tail assembly and associated fairings are similar in appearance to the type used on the North American's F-86 design.* (Rogers Collection, circa 1996)

RACEPLANE TECH
S E R I E S

Project engineer Dick Aley snapped this shot of a beautiful unpainted Miss Ashley II *on one of her first flights.* (Dick Aley, circa 1996)

The engine was run up for the first time is September 1996. Unfortunately, there was not enough time to get the plane ready for the races that year. (Rogers Collection, circa 1996)

The Lear main wing and horizontal tail were mounted to the fuselage in May 1996. (Rogers Collection, circa 1996)

Miss Ashley II *pilot Gary Levitz' racing career dated back to the early 1970s when he was racing his modified Lockheed P-38 Lightning. He also raced North American P-51 Mustangs for many years and was one of the few pilots to fly an F-86 in a Mojave jet races. In 1991, Gary Levitz won the Reno Silver Trophy Race.* (Paul Neuman, circa 1997)

Gary Levitz posing with Miss Ashley II *just prior to the 1998 Reno Gold Race.* (A. Kevin Grantham, circa 1998)

RENO 1997

On September 8, 1997, a beautiful red and white airplane with race number 38 on its tail appeared over Stead Field. The Levitz/Rogers racer now carried the name *Miss Ashley II* after Gary Levitz' daughter, and from the beginning was one of the most attractive air racers to ever adorn the Reno/Stead pit area. Spectator's and race pilots alike came by and marveled over the workmanship that had gone into the purpose-built craft. Each panel on the airplane was custom built and fitted in order to reduce any mismatch. Crew Chief Hank Puckett and his team members were also quick to point out that no surface fillers were used in this airplane's construction. In addition, race number 38 was very well balanced and was completely void of ballast. The National Advisory Committee for Aeronautics (NACA) style air intake also garnished a great deal of attention.

NACA originally designed the more streamlined flush-fitting air intake for jet or high-speed applications in the late 1940s. This technology was tested on the North American YF-93;

however, it was never adopted by the aircraft industry. John Sandberg attempted to use the NACA air intake on his custom-built air racer *Tsunami*. The intake seemed to be streamlined enough, but Sandberg could never get sufficient ram air through the scoop to make it worthwhile. However, that's not the case when it comes to *Miss Ashley II*. Dick Aley, one of the team's engineers, paid close attention to the NACA figures and carefully designed an intake that works very well. Bob Manelski recalls, "Flat out we ran 3,050 revolutions per minute (rpm) and about 98 inches of manifold pressure (MP). Interestingly enough, we gained about 12 inches of MP (in a dive of 3,000 feet per minute or greater) due to the ram effect in the NACA scoop. This put us at 100

inches plus, coming down the chute at the start of the race."

The seven-day Reno race week is broken into three parts. The first three days (Monday-Wednesday) are reserved for pilots of all racing classes to practice flying their respective pylon courses and post speeds that will qualify them for the upcoming races. During the next three days (Thursday-Saturday) race pilots participate in a series of heat races. Sunday, which is the last day of the event, is the culmination of the previous six days when pilots compete for the Bronze, Silver, and Gold trophies.

During the qualifying days, Levitz flew *Miss Ashley II* every morning to get familiar with the airplane's sys-

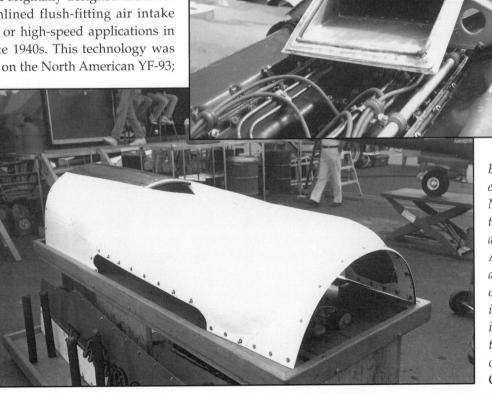

Bill Rogers and project engineer Dick Aley used NACA technical reports to develop a NACA type air intake for Miss Ashley II. *Great attention was paid to overall dimensions of the intake and transition to insure efficient airflow to the throat of the carburetor. (A. Kevin Grantham, circa 1999)*

Miss Ashley II made her debut at the Reno Air Races in 1997. Racer #38 was registered with the Federal Aviation Administration in the experimental class as NX57LR. The number "57" was used as a tribute to Roscoe Turner (who happens to be one of Bill's heroes) as well as to signify that Miss Ashley II is truly a Heinz 57 airplane. The letters "LR" trailing the "57" stand for Levitz/Rogers. (A. Kevin Grantham)

tems and radio data back to his crew. This data was then used to develop a baseline calibration for balancing engine power settings with water injection and spray bar flow rates. A cold engine puts out less power, whereas a hot one might overheat and detonate, so racing teams strive to find the delicate balance that will produce the optimum power from their engine.

The first few days at Reno were trying times for the *Miss Ashley II* crew. One water setting would cool the engine too much and the next wouldn't cool it enough. However, these little so-called "bugs" were not unexpected. Bill Rogers and Gary Levitz had been around racing enough to know that time and expe-

rience would eventually bring all the pieces together. Each day the plane flew a little faster until finally qualifying at 392.375 mph.

Levitz' qualifying speed earned him a spot in Thursday's Silver Heat race. Unfortunately, he experienced some difficulty in retracting the landing gear shortly after takeoff. Earlier in the week Levitz had similar difficulties with the main gear doors. The team examined and tested the retraction systems and really didn't find any specific problems. It was thought that possibly *Miss Ashley II's* landing gear hydraulic pump wasn't strong enough to overcome the pressure from the air flowing into the aircraft's wheel wells. This minor problem was easily fixed by

applying a steeper takeoff angle and, thereby, using the force of air on the bottom of the wing to help push the gear doors closed. Another possibility was that the lightweight main doors were flexing which caused the microswitch, feeding the cockpit indicator lights, to open. Apparently, the problem of closing the wheel covers persisted in spite of a steeper takeoff angle, but nevertheless Levitz managed to join his fellow competitors in time to start the Silver Heat Race. However, the uncertainty about his gear situation kept him from running the plane at high power, and he finished the race next to last. *Miss Ashley II's* slow showing in the Silver competition resulted in Levitz being bumped down to Friday's Unlimited Bronze Heat.

Results – Heat 1A Silver – 6 Laps
Thursday, September 11, 1997

Racer #	Pilot	Type	Name	Race Time	Speed (mph)
45	Bill Rheinschild	P-51D	*Risky Business*	8:14.57	394.929
55	Sherman Smoot	P-51D	*Voodoo Chile*	8:15.23	394.402
66	Nelson Ezell	Sea Fury	*Fury*	8:18.06	392.161
19	Dennis Sanders	Sea Fury	*Argonaut*	8:18.71	391.650
11	Brent N. Hisey	P-51D	*Miss America*	9:53.45	329.126
38	Gary Levitz	P-51R	*Miss Ashley II*	9:37.85	313.694*
10	Skip Holm	Sea Fury	*Critical Mass*	8:37.85	313.694**

* Completed 5 laps.
** Moved to last place by Contest Committee for dead-line cut.

Results – Heat 2C Bronze – 6 Laps
Friday, September 12, 1997

Racer #	Pilot	Type	Name	Race Time	Speed (mph)
38	Gary Levitz	P-51R	*Miss Ashley II*	8:05.15	402.597
105	Stewart Dawson	Sea Fury	*Spirit of Texas*	9:17.98	350.048
11	Brent N. Hisey	P-51D	*Miss America*	9:30.33	342.468
12	James Michaels	P-51D	*Queen 'B'*	9:31.35	341.857
2	Thomas Camp	Yak 11	*Maniyak*	9:35.54	339.368
204	Alan Preston	P-51D	———	8:19.51	325.212*
68	William Anders	P-51D	*Val-Halla*	8:24.50	321.995*
71	Robert Converse	P-51D	*Huntress III*	9:05.97	297.538*

* Completed 5 laps.

Racer #	Pilot	Type	Name	Race Time	Speed (mph)
7	Bill Destefani	P-51D	*Strega*	7:11.23	452.936
77	Lyle Shelton	Bear Cat	*Rare Bear*	7:18.58	445.346
8	Brian Sanders	Sea Fury	*Dreadnought*	7:32.75	431.408
38	Gary Levitz	P-51R	*Miss Ashley II*	8:05.85	401.017
66	Howard Pardue	Sea Fury	*Fury*	8:12.94	396.234
45	Bill Rheinschild	P-51D	*Risky Business*	8:17.98	392.224
19	Dennis Sanders	Sea Fury	*Argonaut*	8:20.21	390.476
10	Skip Holm	Sea Fury	*Critical Mass*	8:25.75	386.198

It is not uncommon to see racing teams burning the midnight oil at Reno. (A. Kevin Grantham, circa 1998)

Results – Gold Trophy Race – 8 Laps
Sunday, September 14, 1997

Racer #	Pilot	Type	Name	Race Time	Speed (mph)
7	Bill Destefani	P-51D	*Strega*	9:36.14	453.130
8	Brian Sanders	Sea Fury	*Dreadnought*	9:41.36	441.467
77	Lyle Shelton	Bearcat	*Rare Bear*	10:16.00	423.809**
38	Gary Levitz	P-51R	*Miss Ashley II*	10:30.10	414.325
45	Bill Rheinschild	P-51D	*Risky Business*	10:32.99	412.433
15	Lloyd Hamilton	Sea Fury	*Furias*	9:39.42	393.830*
20	Daniel Martin	P-51D	*Ridge Runner*	9:52.63	385.051*
66	Howard Pardue	Sea Fury	*Fury*	9:53.55	364.455
76	Matt Jackson	Sea Fury	*Southern Cross*	10:02.34	378.844

* 7 Laps completed.
** Cut outer 6 pylon on lap 3, plus 16 seconds penalty.

After putting in some long hours to resolve the previous day's gear retraction difficulties the Bronze Heat 2C proved to be an exciting race for the crew of the Levitz/Rogers racer. Gary Levitz maneuvered into the last starting position as the eight-plane element lined-up for the race. Then Steve Hinton, in the pace plane, gave the go ahead to start the race. Levitz pushed the power up and managed to take the first pylon and easily out-distanced the competition to capture a first-place finish with a speed of 402.597 mph.

Friday's first-place finish was fast enough to push *Miss Ashley II* up into Saturday's Gold Heat, in which she placed fourth behind the pre-race favorites of *Strega*, *Rare Bear*, and *Dreadnought*.

Sunday's Gold Race began much as these races had in the past, with *Strega* taking the early lead in front of *Rare Bear*. Slowly but surely, *Strega* increased the lead as the *Bear* fell back. Lyle Shelton reported a rough engine over the radio after being overtaken by *Dreadnought*. Gary Levitz pushed *Miss Ashley II's* stock Griffon a little harder, without engaging the high blower (72 inches of manifold pressure at 3,000 rpm), and flew a very nice consistent race and again managed to place fourth, behind the trio of *Strega*, *Dreadnought*, and *Rare Bear*, with an average speed of 414.325 mph. Then the real drama began.

Rear Bear's engine was getting worse and then suddenly lost all power. A "Mayday" was called and Lyle Shelton opted to land on Runway 18 due to the heavy crosswinds. In the meantime, *Strega* and pilot Bill "Tiger" Destefani were also in trouble. *Strega's* canopy was covered with oil that came from a leaking prop seal. Tiger, too, opted to land on Runway 18, but came down a bit hard and the prop struck the ground several times before the damaged Mustang finally rolled to a stop near *Rare Bear*. The rest of the Gold competitors landed safely.

Coming to the national air races with an untried, purpose-built airplane and finishing in the top five is a very significant accomplishment. Reno '97 was supposed to be just a shakedown event for the Levitz/Rogers organization, but finishing fourth in the prestigious Gold Race planted seeds of confidence and raised the racing team's expectations for 1998.

Reno 1998

During the off season, Bill Rogers and his crew began to incorporate some of the lessons learned during the previous year. Improvements planned for *Miss Ashley II* included improving the aircraft's aerodynamics and boosting its engine power.

The original aluminum main landing gear doors were replaced with stronger and more aerodynamic carbon fiber types. Attention was also directed toward the leading edge of the wing. The original Lear wing was patterned from the wings used on the Swiss P.16 fighter. However, the leading edge was changed somewhat to give the private jet better low-speed landing characteristics. Race pilots are used to going fast and flying airplanes that are not as docile as most, so Rogers went about looking for someone to fabricate his new wing components. Crewmembers Sheryl and Greg Kerkof contacted some friends in the hydroplane business whom eventually produced the new, space-age looking leading edges out of carbon fiber.

Adding a nitrous oxide injection system to Racer 38's beefy Griffon was probably the most significant change made to *Miss Ashley II* in 1998. Nitrous oxide (N2O), more commonly know as laughing gas, is a stable compound consisting of two nitrogen atoms and one oxygen atom. This compound was used as a source of oxygen in power-boosting piston engines in World War II. As one might expect, all forms of motor sports, including air racing, quickly adopted this technology. *Miss Ashley II*, like most racing craft, is not that roomy, so the area behind the pilot's seat had to be redesigned to accommodate the two nitrous bottles. Crew Chief Hank Puckett moved the location of the oxygen bottle and built some trick brackets to hold the nitrous cylinders. Hank Puckett also built the nitrous injection control that injects both liquid nitrous oxide and extra fuel through a nozzle in the blower. The nitrous liquid soon turns to gas when it leaves the nozzle and the oxygen-rich fuel mixture rapidly increases the power output of the engine.

As race week approached, the word circulated that both perennial champions, "Tiger" Destefani and Lyle Shelton, would definitely miss the 1998 competition due to the damage their aircraft incurred in 1997. (*Rare Bear's* exhaust ring broke and burnt a portion of the aircraft cowling. Destefani's P-51 suffered a damaged propeller and wing as the result of his hard emergency landing.) Specu-

Miss Ashley II's landing gear was a hybrid design that included Aerostar upper trunnions, Piper Cheyenne lower forks, Cessna 421 retractable Struts and Cessna Caravan wheels with Gulfstream nose wheel tires. (A. Kevin Grantham, circa 1998)

lation among air race enthusiasts was rampant in regards to who would step up and be the next national champion. *Miss Ashley II* had already won the award for the best looking air racer, and with the new modifications — well, time would tell.

As in 1997, the Levitz/Rogers crew was hard at work the first few days of the 35th Annual National Championship Air Races. Each morning one could hear the distinctive Griffon growl over Stead Field as Levitz made calibration flights in preparation for the racing events. On the first day of qualifying, Levitz posted an average speed of 429.378 mph, which is almost a 40-mph improvement over his 1997 speed. A few days later, Levitz jumped up to the number three starting position with an official qualifying speed of 437.376 mph. Racing pit spectators had heard the rumors that *Miss Ashley II* might finally use the high blower with nitrous injection, but the crew wasn't talking.

The top three qualifiers in Unlimited Class — *Voodoo*, *Dago Red*, and *Miss Ashley II* — were given the day off on Thursday, so the Levitz/Rogers crew used the time to get ready for Friday's showdown. The Unlimited Heat 2A Gold Race (5 Laps) was the heat race that most of the unlimited fans had been waiting for as the three top qualifiers lined up on the pace plane. Gary Levitz once again experienced a problem with his gear doors, so he maneuvered his racer to the end of the starting lineup. Bob Hannah in *Voodoo* took a short-lived lead in the race until Bruce Lockwood piloting *Dago Red* passed him on the backside of the course. Shortly thereafter, both racers pulled back on the power to save their engines for Sunday. However, Dennis Sanders in *Dreadnought* kept up the pressure so Lockwood again applied power. Levitz' gear door problem became more acute as the damaged carbon fiber door left the plane and fell to the desert below. The exposed wheel well caused considerable drag, and Levitz wisely didn't stress his Griffon in a race he could not win.

For the second time in as many years, a problem with a gear door had cost the *Miss Ashley II* team a race. Back on the ground, the problems were quickly sorted out. The older 1997 type main landing gear doors were substituted for the new lighter doors and by early Saturday morning, Racer 38 was ready for the Unlimited Gold Heat 3C that had moments of both extreme excitement and terror.

Starboard gear door of Miss Ashley II *lists the dedicated crew that brought this Griffon-powered racer to life.* (A. Kevin Grantham)

Results – Heat 2A Gold – 5 Laps
Friday, September 18, 1998

Racer #	Pilot	Type	Name	Race Time	Speed (mph)
4	Bruce Lockwood	P-51D	*Dago Red*	6:21.42	430.931
5	Bob Hannah	P-51D	*Voodoo*	6:25.02	426.902
8	Dennis Sanders	Sea Fury	*Dreadnought*	6:25.78	426.061
86	Sherman Smoot	Yak 11	*Czech Mate*	6:59.57	391.748
38	Gary Levitz	P-51D	*Miss Ashley II*	7:17.00	376.123*
45	Matt Jackson	P-51D	*Risky Business*	7:29.45	365.704

* Cut Outer 6 Pylon on lap 5, +10 seconds penalty.

All three of the top qualifiers were lined up and ready to go when Steve Hinton, flying a Lockheed T-33 pace plane, called the start of the race. *Dago Red* took the early lead over *Voodoo* and *Miss Ashley II*. Then *Voodoo* very abruptly pulled up; however, pilot Bob Hannah didn't radio a distress call. Then Sherman Smoot's *Czech Mate* belched flames and smoke. Smoot pulled off the course and immediately called a "Mayday." Smoot's Yak doesn't glide very well, so he brought the plane down at about 170 mph and ground looped it at the end of the runway. The gear collapsed and the Yak slid sideways for a good distance before stopping just short of a small bluff on the eastern side of the airport. Smoot quickly jumped out of the plane and walked away a very lucky man.

In the meantime, Steve Hinton flew over to take a look at *Voodoo*. "You OK Bob?" called Hinton. "Yea, this thing just popped big time," replied Hannah. What Hannah didn't mention is that the g-load from the quick pull-up had caused him to black out. He finally managed to reach the throttle and reduced *Voodoo's* power. At that point, Hannah radioed that he "wasn't out of it yet," but he wasn't thinking clearly. Later, he declared a "Mayday" and made a perfect landing. The race continued

The new cowling needed a little customizing before it was ready for the final assembly. (Bill Rogers Collection, circa 1996)

Results – Heat 3A Gold – 5 Laps
Saturday, September 19, 1998

Racer #	Pilot	Type	Name	Race Time	Speed (mph)
4	Bruce Lockwood	P-51D	*Dago Red*	6:12.402	441.369
8	Dennis Sanders	Sea Fury	*Dreadnought*	6:25.78	439.551
38	Gary Levitz	P-51R	*Miss Ashley II*	6:23.39	428.717
45	Bill Rheinschild	P-51D	*Risky Business*	6:43.83	407.017
114	Brian Sanders	Sea Fury	*Argonaut*	7:22.98	371.045
86	Sherman Smoot	Yak 11	*Czech Mate*	DNF	
5	Bob Hannah	P-51D	*Voodoo*	DNF	

as *Dago Red* narrowly edged *Dreadnought* for the win. *Miss Ashley II* also had its best race performance to date with an average speed of 428.717 mph. After the race, one could see what caused *Voodoo's* problems. The left elevator linkage failed when the elevator trim-tab fluttered and departed the plane. Fortunately, Bob Hannah's skill and coolness in the cockpit saved the day.

On Sunday the Levitz/Rogers clan was very optimistic about its chances in the upcoming race. With a week's worth of competition behind the competitors, it was finally time to see three of the four top qualifiers push the throttle home. The race had a very frightening beginning when the engine in Howard Pardue's Sea Fury sputtered on takeoff. One could hear the record crowd of spectators take a deep breath as their heartbeat moved to their throats. He was able to get the engine running again while gaining a little altitude before turning left and executing an excellent emergency landing. Pardue certainly had his hands full for a few moments, but he sure made it look easy.

Lockwood was first on the course after Hinton called, "Gentlemen you have a race," but he was soon overtaken by Dennis Sanders in *Dread-nought*. Sanders had the inside position, flying very tight and low on the course. Gary Levitz was a close third when he radioed back to his pit that something had just struck the canopy, and that the temperature gauges in the cockpit pegged. Levitz

A typical start of the Gold Race. All of the racers form up line abreast until the pace plane puts them into a shallow dive before releasing the competitors down the so-called "chute" on to the racecourse. (A. Kevin Grantham, circa 1998)

Miss Ashley II's 1998 crew. Back row L-R: Bill Rogers, Sheryl and Greg Kerkof, Brett Wilson, Mike Gullikson, Hank Puckett, Bob Manelski, Mike Wilson, Bob Rogers (Bill's Dad), John Brooks, Lance Paxton and Dale Stolzer. Front row L-R: Gary Levitz, Deanna Manelski, Dick Aley, Mike Levitz (Gary's son), and Gayle Paxton. (Paul Neuman)

pulled back on the power a bit and fell behind Bill Rheinschild's P-51D *Risky Business*. *Miss Ashley II's* crew couldn't tell what had happened, but the airplane seemed to be all right with the single exception of the high reading temperature gauges, so Levitz pressed the nitrous button during the second lap. The nitrous oxide fuel mixture boosted the engine power to approximately 4,000 horsepower and *Miss Ashley II* leaped past *Risky Business*. During lap three, Lockwood got caught in the propwash of the big Sea Fury as they approached Pylon Two. For a moment, it looked like *Dago Red* might flip over, but Lockwood is a

fine pilot, and he managed the situation and eventually passed *Dreadnought* and sprinted to the finish line. *Miss Ashley II* also had a very nice race. However, Gary Levitz cut Pylon 4 on the first lap, and the ensuing penalty vaulted Bill Rheinschild to third place.

After the race a blood trail was discovered on *Miss Ashley II's* cowling. Presumably a Seagull had met its untimely end after being sucked through the NACA air intake and swallowed by the hungry Mk. 58 Griffon. A bit of bad luck for the team but, nevertheless, they felt that their 1998 racing campaign was a

successful one and now it was time to focus on the future. "As if the bird weren't enough, photos of the race showed that the gear door indicator lights were not mistaken and in fact the right inboard door was open about an inch, causing tremendous drag," said Bob Manelski. "Once we got back to Seattle we had to prepare to ferry the airplane to the 1998 NBAA convention in Las Vegas. As part of this preparation, a compression check was done which revealed that we had run the Gold race on about 10 cylinders. In the ensuing three weeks between Reno and NBAA, we painted the fuselage, and changed the engine."

Results – Gold Trophy Race – 7 Laps
Sunday, September 20, 1998

Racer #	Pilot	Type	Name	Race Time	Speed (mph)
4	Bruce Lockwood	P-51D	*Dago Red*	8:30.68	450.599
8	Dennis Sanders	Sea Fury	*Dreadnought*	8:36.75	445.306
45	Bill Rheinschild	P-51D	*Risky Business*	9:07.14	420.572
38	Gary Levitz	P-51R	*Miss Ashley II*	9:19.25	411.465*
114	Brian Sanders	Sea Fury	*Argonaut*	9:45.45	392.375
105	Stewart Dawson	Sea Fury	*Spirit of Texas*	8:34.56	383.316**
74	Matt Jackson	Sea Fury	*Bad Attitude*	8:40.03	379.284**
66	Howard Pardue	Sea Fury	*Fury*	DNF	

* Cut Outer Pylon 4 on lap 1, +14 seconds penalty
** Time computed on 8 laps completed.

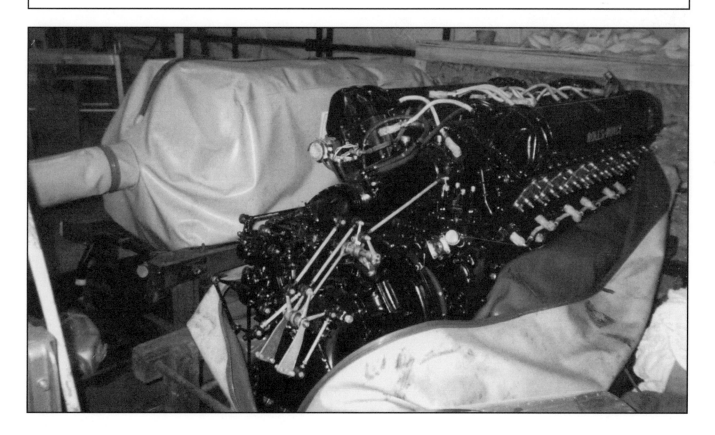

Two of the Rolls-Royce Griffon 58 engines that were acquired in England. (Bill Rogers Collection, circa 1996)

Reno 1999

Most racing teams attempt to improve their racer's performance each year by forming various engine and aerodynamic modifications. The Levitz/Rogers racing team captured the imagination of everyone in 1999 by making the most innovative changes to its racing plane.

During the 1998 race, "Tiger" Destefani was a frequent visitor to the *Miss Ashley II* pit area. During one of these visits, Tiger mentioned how he had increased *Strega's* top speed by cutting down the frontal profile and stretching out the length of its coolant scoop. Bill Rogers already knew about the benefits of a more streamlined scoop, but in previous

years didn't have the time to pursue it. When time finally presented itself, Rogers took the idea a few steps further than just reducing the scoop area.

The success of *Miss Ashley II's* NACA air intake fostered the notion of using the same technology on the coolant scoop. Soon team engineer Dick Aley was hard at work calculating the dimensions of the proposed coolant duct. The old *Georgia Mae* coolant housing and radiators were removed and drawings were made for the new NACA carbon fiber scoop. When finished, the actual composite assembly weighed only 63 pounds. Its design also allowed the radiator and oil cooler to be positioned deeper inside *Miss Ashley*

II's fuselage, giving way to a more streamlined profile. Subsequent test flights performed by Skip Holm proved the efficiency of the NACA adaptation, and the aircraft's performance numbers went up, as well. Along the way, Rogers and Aley also came up with the idea of using vortex generators to uniformly steer the cooling air up and through the radiator. Another outgrowth of the new scoop was additional space that could be used to add two more nitrous bottles, doubling *Miss Ashley II's* nitrous oxide capacity.

Gary Levitz departed Everett, Washington, on his way to Reno on the Friday before race week, 1999. Along the way the prop-seal began to leak oil that ended up on the windscreen,

Side view of the new scoop and radiator setup. The new arrangement gave way for more room to double Miss Ashley II's *nitrous oxide capacity.* (A. Kevin Grantham, circa 1999)

and Levitz was forced to land at Eugene, Oregon. Bill Rogers and some of the team members hurried, changed their commercial flight plans and flew to Eugene to repair the leaking propeller. At the same time, Levitz called his general manager John Brooks and assigned him the task of finding a replacement seal. For a while, the whole ordeal was beginning to resemble a circus, but in the end a new seal was found, and by Sunday *Miss Ashley II* was once again stabled in her familiar Reno pit area.

Unfortunately, the repairs that got the plane to Reno were just a momentary solution because the leaking prop seal continued to plague the crew during the first two days of the qualifying rounds. In addition, the coolant system didn't seem to work well enough to keep the big engine cool. Each day different spray bar flow rates were used, and every time the results were less than desirable. Finally on Tuesday, Levitz qualified for the races at 430.717 mph. On the last day of qualifying, Levitz once again entered the course and put the hammer down until he encountered slower traffic. He decided then to pull off the course and wait for the slower airplanes to complete their runs before reentering the time trials. Levitz radioed to his crew that the engine was still getting hot. Unfortunately, the ADI system circuit breaker popped before the racecourse cleared, and Levitz was forced to abort his final attempt to improve his qualifying position.

Miss Ashley II's official speed was slightly faster than in 1998, and it gave the red and white racer the pole position for Thursday's Unlimited Heat 1A Silver. This race finally produced the results that the

Miss Ashley II's control system was a hybrid combination of Mustang and Lear components. One of the unique aspects of the control setup was the electric trim system controlled by a button on the stick. (A. Kevin Grantham, circa 1997)

Results – Heat 1A Silver – 6 Laps
Thursday, September 16, 1999

Racer #	Pilot	Type	Name	Race Time	Speed (mph)
38	Gary Levitz	P-51R	*Miss Ashley II*	7:38.94	393.214*
114	Dennis Sanders	Sea Fury	*Argonaut*	7:42.90	389.850
105	Nelson Ezell	Sea Fury	*Spirit of Texas*	7:43.29	389.522
911	John Brown	Sea Fury	*September Pops*	7:43.95	388.968
11	Brent N. Hisey	P-51D	*Miss America*	8:13.28	365.840
45	Bill Rheinschild	P-51D	*Risky Business*	7:31.60	333.004**
66	Howard Pardue	Sea Fury	*Fury*	DNF	

* Cut Outer Pylon 3 on Pace lap 1 and Lap 3, plus 24 seconds penalty
** Time computed on 5 laps completed.

Levitz/Rogers crew had been trying to achieve. Overnight they removed the racer's radiator and discovered that its water flow was restricted. "Radiator Dave," from the *Dago Red* racing team, was called in, and by race time the problems with the over-heating engine appeared to be history. Gary Levitz had the pole position, and from the start, poured the coal to the big Griffon engine. *Miss Ashley II* purred around the course and easily established an insurmountable lead over the rest of the pack. Then Gary Levitz radioed back to his crew that he might have cut a pylon. Team member Bob Manelski told Gary that he had better push it up a bit in order to compensate for the potential penalty. Meanwhile, Dennis Sanders, Nelson Ezell, and John Brown were fighting it out for second place. Three Sea Furies flew in tight racing formation, followed by Brent Hisey in *Miss America*. Bill Rheinschild's P-51D *Risky Business*, flying on its fifth

engine in as many days, never really got in the competition.

After the race, it was announced that Levitz had, in fact, cut pylon three twice during the race, but it really didn't matter in the end because Levitz still had four seconds to spare after the 24-second penalty (two seconds per pylon times six laps) was assessed. Team member Bob Manelski recalled, "He won the '99 Sliver Race on Thursday in his own words, 'loafing — I could fly like this all day' at 2,750 rpm, with 75 inches manifold pressure, leaving about 400 hp to spare; not to mention, another 500-plus available in nitrous." The win on Thursday provided the bump that the Levitz/Rogers racer needed to get back into Gold Class competition. But problems in Friday's heat race would once again keep *Miss Ashley II* from reaching her full potential.

The Heat 3A Gold match-up of the

top three qualifiers had long been anticipated by the Reno race fans. *Strega* took the early lead ahead of *Dago Red*. *Rare Bear* struck a bird and pilot Matt Jackson had to "Mayday" out of the race in the first lap. Gary Levitz also had to leave the race during the second lap with electrical problems. Bruce Lockwood continued to press the leader by flying a very nice, high, but tight race and eventually overtook *Strega* to easily win the heat. Brian Sanders and his reliable Sea Fury battleship, known as *Dreadnought*, came in third. Tom Dwelle's Sea Fury *Critical Mass* and Dan Martin's Mustang *Ridge Runner* rounded out the top finishers.

A chaffed wire that shorted out the generator and two voltage regulators caused *Miss Ashley II's* electrical problem. Gary Levitz was never in any real danger but he didn't feel comfortable continuing the race with just battery power.

Racer #	Pilot	Type	Name	Race Time	Speed (mph)
4	Bruce Lockwood	P-51D	*Dago Red*	6:35.35	456.461
7	Bill Destefani	P-51D	*Strega*	6:40.58	450.501
8	Brian Sanders	Sea Fury	*Dreadnought*	6:57.73	432.006
10	Tom Dwelle	Sea Fury	*Critical Mass*	7:03.60	426.019
20	Daniel Martin	P-51D	*Ridge Runner*	6:48.82	367.851*
38	Gary Levitz	P-51R	*Miss Ashley II*	DNF Lap 2	
77	Matt Jackson	Bearcat	*Rare Bear*	DNF Lap 1	

* Time computed on 5 laps completed.

Gary Levitz was able to stay in the Gold Unlimited racing class in spite of not finishing Friday's heat race. Overnight, new electrical components were installed and the following morning *Miss Ashley II* was once again ready for competition.

Eight speedy unlimited racers were lined abreast just north of Stead Field. Each pilot holding his starting position as the pace plane led them into a shallow dive to start the Gold Heat Race. *Strega*, hotly followed by *Dago Red*, was the first airplane to enter the racecourse. Gary Levitz and *Miss Ashley II* held seventh place behind two Sea Furies and two Mustangs as the spread-out pack of racing airplanes sped past the home pylon. Then suddenly a loud cracking noise was heard as *Miss Ashley II's* tail section separated from the craft just as Levitz appeared to be setting up his turn on Pylon Two. The tailless *Miss Ashley II* pitched down slightly, then rolled over and

In 1999, Bill Rogers decided to take the NACA Duct application a step further by using it as a coolant scoop. The resulting scoop assembly was made out of lightweight carbon fiber material. The redesigned air intake also opened up additional space in the lower fuselage which was used to house two additional Nitrous Oxide bottles. This view of the bottom side of the aircraft gives one the notion that the finely tapered NACA duct simply invites the cooling air to pass through the system. (A. Kevin Grantham)

Gary Levitz basks in the applause of more than 50,000 spectators who always enjoyed seeing the veteran race. (Nicholas A. Veronico)

fell to the ground claiming the life of veteran race pilot Gary Levitz.

The loss of Gary Levitz and what he brought to the sport of air racing will not soon be forgotten. Levitz in one way or another touched every member of the Levitz/Rogers racing team, and many of the crewmembers feel that Gary would want them to continue with another racing project. It perhaps is best to close this volume by saying that this is but one chapter of possibly many that is yet to be written about the racing team that was assembled by Bill Rogers and Gary Levitz.

Miss Ashley II will no doubt be remembered for being one the most beautiful and innovative airplanes to have ever graced the Reno Air Races. Blue Skies Forever Gary! (A. Kevin Grantham)

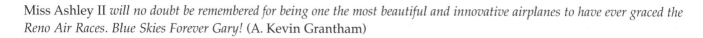

This view of Miss Ashley II *clearly shows her Mustang and Lear origins.* (A. Kevin Grantham, circa 1998)

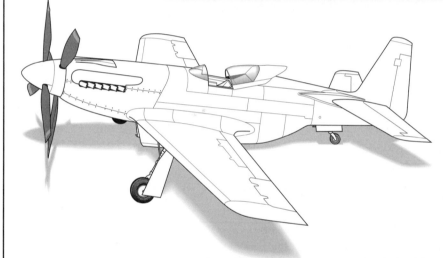

Walk-around view of Miss Ashley II. (Brett Wilson)

Bruce Lockwood's Dago Red *captured the Gold Trophy in 1998 and 1999.* (A. Kevin Grantham)

Racer 38 was equipped with a stock Avro Shackleton propeller and spinner setup. This photograph was taken in 1997 at Reno shortly before the "II" was added to Miss Ashley II. *(A. Kevin Grantham)*

Gary Levitz rounding pylon 2 on the Reno racecourse in 1997. Levitz was well known for flying a high but very tight course. The speeds achieved around the racetrack typically averaged between 420-450 mph. (A. Kevin Grantham)

Bill Rogers' original concept for a Griffon-powered racing airplane combined the classic lines of the Supermarine Mk.XIV Spitfire with a cut-down canopy and a tall P-51H vertical tail. (Bill Rogers' original redrawn by Brett Wilson)

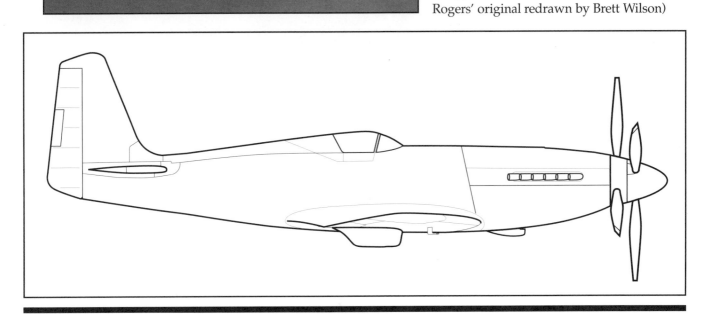

The brightly polished unpainted airframe clearly gives one an idea of the type of workmanship that went into building Miss Ashley II. (Bill Rogers)

THE NACA DUCT

The NACA duct was first used on the North American YF-93. This new air intake showed promise; however, it was never adopted by the aircraft industry as a primary intake system. (USAF photo via Dave Ostrowski)

Developed by the old National Advisory Committee on Aeronautics, NACA ducts present a flat surface to the approaching airflow that largely eliminates the scoop as a source of drag; however, it still leaves the internal ducting and cooling components to be dealt with. Although it is ideal to place a NACA duct near the front of a surface, where the boundary layer is thin and laminar, this cannot always be achieved due to other design requirements. The edges of the duct must be sharp, allowing the airflow to roll up around these edges to form a vortex along each side — the pressure differentials of the vortices help draw air into the duct. NACA ducts are frequently used on race cars and aircraft for small volume cooling flows such as brake or oil cooling.

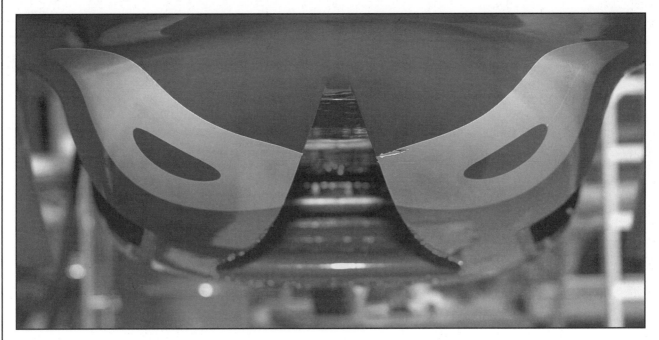

Miss Ashley II arrived at Reno in 1999 with a brand new NACA-type coolant duct replacing the normal belly-scoop used on other P-51s. This sexy new scoop worked very well while small internal vortex generators helped uniformly steer the airflow to the coolant radiator. (A. Kevin Grantham)

BIBLIOGRAPHY

SOURCES AND SUGGESTED FURTHER READING

Berliner, Don. *Unlimited Air Racers: The Complete History of Unlimited Class Air Racing, 1946 Thompson Trophy to 1991 Reno Gold.* Motorbooks International. Osceola, Wisconsin. 1992.

Carter, Dustin W. and Birch J. Matthews. *Mustang: The Racing Thoroughbred.* Schiffer Military History. West Chester, Pennsylvania. 1992.

Coggin, Paul A. *Mustang Survivors.* Aston Publications. Bourne End, Bucks, England. 1987.

Grantham, A. Kevin. *"P-Screamers: The History of the Surviving Lockheed P-38 Lightnings."* Pictorial Histories Publishing. Missoula, Montana. 1993.
_____. *"Air Racing Historians Gather In Cleveland."* In Flight Aviation News. July 1992.
_____. *"Racing P-38s."* Presentation to the Society of Air Racing Historians. 1993.
_____, and Tim Weinschenker. *"1946 Cleveland National Air Races."* Presentation to the Society of Air Racing Historians. 1994.
_____, and Tim Weinschenker. *"1947 Cleveland National Air Races."* Presentation to the Society of Air Racing Historians. 1995.
_____, and Tim Weinschenker. *"1948 Cleveland National Air Races."* Presentation to the Society of Air Racing Historians. 1996.
_____, and Tim Weinschenker. *"1949 Cleveland National Air Races."* Presentation to the Society of Air Racing Historians. 1997.
_____, and Jackie Grantham. *"Unlimiteds Thunder At Reno '97."* Avweb.
http://www.avweb.com/articles/reno97.html
_____, and Jackie Grantham. *"Reno Unlimiteds Turn 35."* Avweb.
http://www.avweb.com/articles/reno98.html
_____, and Jackie Grantham. "Reno Report '97." *Warbirds Worldwide.* Issue 43.
_____, and Jackie Grantham. "Reno '98." *Warbirds Worldwide.* Issue 47.
_____, and Jackie Grantham. "Reno '99." *Warbirds Worldwide.* Issue 51.
_____, and Jackie Grantham. "Levitz-Rogers Racer." *Warbirds Worldwide.* Issue 38.
_____, and Jackie Grantham. "Miss Ashley II Update." *Warbirds Worldwide.* Issue 43.

Kinert, Reed. *Racing Planes and Air Races.* Various editions. Aero Publishers. Fallbrook, California. 1972,

Larsen, Jim. *Directory of Unlimited Class Pylon Air Racers.* American Air Museum. Kirkland, Washington. 1971.
_____. "Red Baron's RB-104." *Air Classics.* April 1977.
_____. "Year of the Red Baron." *Air Classics.* February 1978.

O'Leary, Michael. "Races, Records, and Disaster." *Air Classics.* February 1974.

Tegler, John. *"Gentlemen, You Have A Race:" A History of the Reno National Championship Air Races 1964-1983.* Wings Publishing. Severna Park, Maryland. 1984.
_____. "Who's On First?" *Air Classics.* February 1975.
_____. "Unlimiteds At Mojave." *Air Classics.* October 1975.
_____. "Heavy Metal At Reno." *Air Classics.* January 1976.
_____. "Mustangs Over Mojave." *Air Classics.* November 1976.
_____. "Bang! The Unlimiteds at the 1976 Reno National Air Races." *Air Classics.* January 1977.
_____. "Unlimiteds Over Reno." *Air Classics.* January 1979.
_____. "The R.B. Reigns Supreme." *Air Classics.* March 1979.
_____. "Racers Over Mojave." *Air Classics.* October 1979.
_____. "Phoenix Rising?" *Air Classics.* August 1995.

Veronico, Nicholas A. *F4U Corsair: The Combat, Development, and Racing History of the Corsair.* Motorbooks International. Osceola, Wisconsin. 1994.
_____. "Whittington Walks Away From 'Precious Metal.'" *In Flight Aviation News.* October 1988.
_____. "Lyle Shelton Wins Unlimited Gold At Reno Races '88." *In Flight Aviation News.* October 1988.
_____. "Rare Bear Does It Again, Wins Reno Gold." *In Flight Aviation News.* October 1989.
_____. "Shelton, Rare Bear Win Third Gold." *In Flight Aviation News.* October 1990.
_____. "Shelton Wins Reno: Fourth Year In A Row." *In Flight Aviation News.* October 1991.
_____. "Strega Wins Unlimited Gold At 29th Reno Races." *In Flight Aviation News.* October 1992.
_____. "Gentlemen — you have a race! Action From Reno." *FlyPast* Magazine. December 1992.
_____. "Fire Breather! Action From The 30th Reno Races." *FlyPast* Magazine. December 1993.